CONFRONTING THE DEMON

Confronting the Demon

A Gospel Response to Adult Bullying

Gerald A. Arbuckle, S.M.

LITURGICAL PRESS
Collegeville, Minnesota

www.litpress.org

Cover design by Ann Blattner.

First published by St. Pauls Publications, 2003

Published in the United States of America and in Canada by the Liturgical Press, Collegeville, Minnesota.

ST. PAULS PUBLICATIONS is an activity of the priests and brothers of the Society of St. Paul who place at the center of their lives the mission of evangelization through the modern means of social communication.

1	2	3	4	5	6	7	8

Library of Congress Cataloging-in-Publication Data

Arbuckle, Gerald A.
   Confronting the demon : a gospel response to adult bullying / Gerald A. Arbuckle.
      p.   cm.
   Includes bibliographical references and index.
   ISBN 0-8146-3016-2 (pbk : alk. paper)
   1. Bullying—Religious aspects—Catholic Church. 2. Christian sociology—Catholic Church. 3. Catholic Church—Doctrines. I. Title.

BX1795.B84A73 2004
261.8'3—dc22

                                                              2003027080

For

The voiceless victims of violence

I am silent; I do not open by mouth…
Hear my prayer, O Lord,
and give ear to my cry;
do not hold your peace at my tears.
For I am your passing guest,
an alien, like all my forebears.

Psalm 39:9, 12

In the face of so much [violence] it's not possible for us
to sit with our hands folded.

St. Teresa of Avila

Acknowledgments

My special thanks to Michael Goonan, S.S.P., and Jane Macduff of St. Pauls Publications for their encouragement to write this book and to Christopher Brennan, S.S.P., for his careful editing; my colleagues Michael Mullins, S.M., Kerry Brettell, Patricia Moroney, and Elaine Richard for their willingness to share their expertise concerning the book's theme; Catherine Duncan for her tireless, detailed reading of, and commenting on, the text; and the many people in workshops around the world who have shared their reflections on experiences of bullying. These people, however, are in no way responsible for any inadequacies in the present book.

Scripture quotations are from the New Revised Standard Version of the Bible, © copyright 1989 by the Division of Christian Education of the National Council of Churches of Christ of the United States of America, and are used with permission.

Gerald A. Arbuckle, S.M.
12 September 2003

Contents

Introduction

By the natural law, every human being has the right to respect for his or her person, to their good reputation, to freedom in searching for truth... He or she has the right ... to be informed truthfully about public events.

Pope John XXIII (1958–1963)[1]

I would like to emphasize that no human right is safe if we fail to commit ourselves to safeguarding all of them. When the violation of any fundamental right is accepted without reaction, all other rights are placed at risk... Every violation of human rights carries within it the seeds of possible conflict.

Pope John Paul II[2]

[Love] means a recognition of the fact that all life is interrelated. All humanity is involved in a single process, and all ... are brothers [sic]. To the degree that I harm my brother [sic], no matter what he [sic] is doing to me, to that extent I am harming myself.

Martin Luther King, Jr.[3]

Bullying is not something confined to school children. It is a widespread form of abuse found in families, workplaces, organizations (including the churches), and beyond, in cultures generally.[4] An authoritative writer on bullying speaks of it as "the hidden epidemic of intentional aggression."[5] Typically, this type of violence involves the abuse of power and provides satisfaction on the part of its perpetrators when they compel victims to submit to them. Further, it causes intimidation that can paralyze the lives and families of victims — and even destroy them.

Bullying is a quality of most forms of violence, including racial, religious, and sex-based discrimination; sexual, physical, and psychological abuse; persecution and terrorism.

This book focuses on the nature and types of contemporary bullying and what the Christian Scriptures advise us to do to prevent it.

The cost and prevalence of bullying

Bullying is extremely costly, both in human and in financial terms. For example, it is estimated that, in 1996, one in eight employees in Britain believed that they had been bullied over the previous five years; in 2000, one in six workers in the United States directly experienced bullying; just over one-half of workers in a recent Australian survey had experienced bullying in the workplace, mostly from their supervisors and managers; and one-third to one-half of all stress-related illnesses in Western societies in general are due to bullying in the workplace. [6]

Economic rationalism, the idea that the ultimate measure of success is only financial profit, is significantly contributing to this type of bullying.[7] Among other things, economic rationalism fosters a culture of sacrifice in which excessive work demands are forced on employees. Such demands adversely affect their own health and welfare and that of their families. Yet, as Pope John XXIII asserted, workers have a fundamental right *not* to be treated as if they were "irrational objects without freedom, to be used at the arbitrary disposition of others."[8] But it is not only employees and their families who suffer: large corporations can collapse, and while directors and executives may walk away with sizable pay-outs, shareholders, including retirees, often fail to retrieve any part of their investments.

Further contemporary examples of bullying

While we all may have experienced intimidation in some form, the following are some further contemporary examples of bullying; they help to provide the context for this book:

• the hurling of abuse by a sectarian mob, in Northern Ireland in September 2001, at crying five-year-old Catholic girls on their way to their first day at school;

• the terrorist attacks which occurred in the United States in September 2001 and in Bali (Indonesia) and Moscow (Russia) in October 2002. While terrorism has been a form of bullying for centuries, modern technology now renders every part of the world vulnerable to its dramatic, fear-evoking power.[9]

• hate crime, a particularly vicious form of bullying which underlay the Holocaust and which has intensified around the world. Such crime is fuelled by the loss of personal and cultural securities and identities, brought on by a globalizing world economy, and encouraged by the rise of right-wing political movements.

Hate crime has been described as "a mechanism of power intended to sustain somewhat precarious hierarchies through violence or threats of violence (verbal or physical). It is generally directed toward those whom societies have traditionally stigmatized and marginalized."[10] Such people include migrants, asylum seekers, women, gay persons, and members of ethnic or religious minorities. However, hate crime does not victimize individuals only: it causes the intimidation of all the members of marginalized groups (see Chapters 2 and 3).

The widespread use of the Internet now enables hate crime to be extended even more — across national boundaries — so facilitating the rise of a potentially global racist subculture (see Chapter 1).[11]

• sexual abuse, a particularly pernicious form of bullying. Ministers of religion are included among its perpetrators, and while the numbers of them involved are relatively small, this in no way lessens the evil of the abuse. The publicity surrounding sexual abuse has uncovered a culture of silence in the churches and this has caused understand-able anger within society.

Within the Catholic Church, such scandals and cover-ups have opened a Pandora's box of grievances and now other instances of perceived victimization are being described more openly. Such instances include the failure of bishops to involve lay persons in decision-making and the maintenance of patriarchal attitudes and structures in ministry and worship.[12] The reluctance of the hierarchy of the Catholic Church to foster Church-wide collaboration, as envisaged by the Second Vatican Council (the second assembly of the Catholic bishops of the world at the Vatican, held over four sessions between 1962 and 1965), is itself an ongoing form of intimidation.

Cultures which promote bullying

The terms "cultures of bullying" and "institutional bullying" refer to cultures which legitimize individuals, institutions, and groups to act in bullying ways. We will briefly examine how they work in Chapter 3 but, for the moment, the following examples illustrate their relevance:

• In the 1980s, the fear of communism in the United States was so prevalent in the culture there that in other countries where the United States exercised influence, people felt encouraged to commit horrendous abuses of human rights to defend right-wing governments. This occurred in Asia and in Nicaragua and El Salvador in Central America. In remarking on Central America, the political commentator Noam Chomsky says that a "prime target of the U.S. [bullying tactics] was the Catholic

Church, which had committed the grievous sin of adopting 'the preferential option for the poor.' "[13]

• In 1999, in Britain, a report into the racist murder of Stephen Lawrence, a black teenager, declared the investigation into his death to have been conducted incompetently.[14] Police had been unwilling to arrest the perpetrators of the crime and had failed to provide information to Lawrence's family. The report attributed the investigators' incompetence to, among other things, a culture of racism among police. Such a culture encouraged individual police to act in bullying ways towards black persons because it failed to hold police accountable for their actions.

• In 2001, the Australian government introduced a policy of turning back refugees from the Indonesian mainland while they were still on the high seas. They had been attempting to reach Australian shores in ill-equipped small boats. This policy, which became widely known internationally, had been condemned by the United Nations.

In August of that year, on the eve of a federal election, Australian television viewers saw pictures purporting to show refugees throwing their children overboard supposedly to force Australian navy ships to rescue and take them to Australia. Politicians claimed this proved such people unworthy of refugee status, yet the children who had been photographed in the water had not been thrown there by other refugees. The truth behind the pictures was withheld until well after the elections.[15]

Such manipulated vilification of anonymous refugees for political advantage was a particularly nasty form of intimidation because the broadcasting of incorrect information helped to reinforce a culture of bullying towards refugees and asylum seekers in Australian society. Further, the refugees could not adequately defend themselves. Editorials in *The Sydney Morning Herald* at the time of the incident reported the disturbing consequences: "Most Australians … are not greatly troubled by the distortions and deceptions the Government resorted to … This is a great pity … [In] a democracy any lie is poison to the system, slow-acting perhaps, but dangerous nonetheless … [The truth's] manipulation is especially insidious when it feeds racism, xenophobia and prejudice."[16]

As well as such manipulation of the truth about refugees, the compulsory detention of asylum seekers, especially of women and children in concentration-camp-like conditions, is a form of ethnic bullying (see Chapter 3).[17] Can we imagine the psychological wounding that people experience in such an environment?

• Caroline Miley, when reviewing her experience in the Anglican Church of Australia, described the Church's culture as one of timidity and of fear of change. This, she claimed, encouraged the marginalization and bullying of those who dare to be innovative in preaching the gospel in a postmodern world.[118]

Bullying: an assault on human dignity

When Pontius Pilate interrogated him, Jesus said: "I came into the world … to testify to the truth" (John 18:37). Truth liberates, and the truth is that every human person is made in the image and likeness of God. Such a likeness is enhanced still further, Christians believe, by the redeeming power of Christ. This is the basis of our dignity; and every act of bullying is an assault on this dignity and the God from whom it comes. Even more so, every act of bullying that remains *unchallenged* in families, governments, businesses, schools, and churches contributes to the development of a wider and more oppressive culture of violence. No Christian or moral person, therefore, can remain an unconcerned bystander when people are abused by others intent on misusing power for their own advantage (see Chapter 4).

Challenging a bully, however, can be a costly experience, as Jesus found. In response to Jesus' reply, Pilate cynically asked: "What is truth?" (John 18:38), then he turned away, continued his abusive behavior, and handed his victim, Jesus, over to his executioners. Like Jesus, moral people are committed to uncovering bullying behavior, but the cost to ourselves is likely to be high. Bullies are never comfortable with the truth and do not encourage it to come to light. Yet learning to identify and prevent the evil of abusive power, which is at the heart of all bullying, is now an absolute prerequisite for human survival. Every failure to challenge the violation of a human right contributes to a local, even worldwide culture in which "all other rights are placed at risk," as John Paul II warns us at the beginning of this Introduction.

The aim and structure of this book

Rather than being a comprehensive study of the social disease referred to as bullying, this short book aims to provide a readable, introductory summary of its nature, meaning, and power, which I hope will stimulate discussion.

In Chapter 1, to overcome confusion about the meaning of the word *bullying*, I define it and explain its nature.

Chapter 2 deals with the qualities of a bully and the impact abuse has on victims.

Chapter 3 looks at the cultural roots of bullying: within every culture, certain types of abusive personality and forms of motivation become accepted and even promoted.

Chapter 4, finally, examines what the Christian Scriptures teach us about the evil of bullying and what we need to do to counteract it in our own lives and the world in which we live.

While the examples and close-ups within the chapters are drawn from a wide variety of countries, workplaces, and sections of society, I have also included questions at the end of each chapter to help us relate the content of the text to our own lives. Again, some of the principles are illustrated by the experience of the Catholic Church, but the book's theme and lessons apply well beyond it to include audiences in general: the book is not intended to be about people "out there" but offers a challenge to us all to examine our own proneness to the vice of bullying.

Chapter 1

Adult Bullying: Definition and Types

Bullying renders the victim impotent: fear paralyses.

Ruth Hadikin[1]

> This chapter explores:
>
> ☞ the meaning of bullying
> ☞ bullying as an abuse of power and an act of violence
> ☞ five common types of bullies in the workplace
> ☞ other types of bullying in the workplace and beyond.

What does "bullying" mean?

The word *bullying* is often used loosely to describe any stressful interaction between peers or between employees and their employers but this matter is not so simple. Employers have the right, for example, to call their employees to account and to do this in a firm yet respectful manner. Employees may find this stressful, but it is not bullying.[2]

Bullying, rather, is "repeated aggression, verbal, psychological or physical, conducted by an individual or a group against others."[3] But even this definition does not go far enough because it fails to state the *purpose* of bullying. This is *to make the perpetrator feel powerful by exploiting the vulnerabilities of their victims.* The following functional definition is fuller; it will be explained and illustrated in this and subsequent chapters. *Bullying* is:

- the *abuse of power* by individuals, groups or institutions,

- driven by *fear of having to face their own inadequacies,*

- so that people (individuals or groups) not in a position to defend themselves are *downgraded as human beings* through being *persistently subjected to threats* or psychological, physical cultural *violence,*

- which *weakens their self-confidence* and self-esteem, so facilitating their subjugation.

Bullies force people to do what they want them to do and will try all kinds of intimidation to achieve this purpose. They seek to dominate their victim(s) for their own gratification and consequently destroy the victim's sense of self-worth. As one researcher comments: "There are parallels between what psychological abusers and torturers do to psychologically break down their victim into submission. The abuser systematically destroys self-confidence and self-esteem over a period of time."[4]

Bullying is possible in *any* group, but particularly in situations which potential victim(s) cannot readily avoid. Obviously, such situations arise in prisons and families, but it is commonly the case for many people in their workplace who cannot change their place of employment easily.[5] Also, members of minority groups, for example, indigenous peoples, migrants, and refugees, are particularly vulnerable to being bullied.

The word *persistently* in our definition needs some explanation. It does not mean that bullying consists simply of a series of abusive actions. On the contrary, only one action may be sufficient to bully others if it brings about an ongoing atmosphere of fear and subjugation. For example, an employer can insult an employee in such a way that the latter is left in dread of yet another abusive outburst. Hence, in such a case, the effects of the one action persist.

Any one bully may intimidate in many different ways too by, for example, using abusive language, passive aggression, physical threats, public or private humiliation, refusing to take the blame for failures, trivial fault-finding, constantly being critical and sarcastic with others, withholding information to maintain power over people, scapegoating, expecting unreasonable results from others, manipulating employers against employees, refusing to delegate authority, and undermining teamwork. Some of these different ways of bullying will be examined later but we need to remember that the contemporary bully's behavior is *not necessarily brutish* or physically threatening. Peter Randall, an authoritative writer on bullying in the workplace, concludes that "bullies can be subtle, charming, intelligent and even sensitive"! He says that "their portrayal of empathy is just a means of preserving their own credibility."[6]

Angela Ishmael, a British consultant on bullying in the workplace, describes how bullying can frequently be disguised or hidden behind excuses and euphemisms in an effort to defend offensive behavior. For example, autocratic styles of management, persistent lateness for appointments, poor interpersonal skills, or personality problems on the part of leaders are often interpreted and tolerated as eccentric behavior when really they amount to bullying because of their persistent effect on victims. Such behavior needs to be named as bullying.[7]

Bullying is an obsessive compulsive behavior, and serial bullies — people who victimize a series of people — need a target onto whom they can project their personal inadequacies and ineptitude and whom they can blame. Other qualities of a bully will be explored in Chapter 2.

Bullying is an abuse of power

As our definition notes, bullying is an abuse of power but, unfortunately, power is popularly understood to mean coercion and domination when it is simply the ability to influence people or events either positively *or* negatively.[8] Power is *positive* when it enables (*em*powers) people to develop their own gifts and those of others; power is *negative* when it involves domination and control of others, for example, in cases of manipulation or coercion.

There are further distinctions concerning power which are worth exploring. The psychologist Rollo May, writing on *positive* power, distinguishes between integrative and nutrient types.[9] *Integrative* power is used when people *share* power with others. For example, people who act non-violently to try to overcome an exploitative style of government and to promote a collaborative form instead are using integrative power. As long as a government refuses an invitation to be more collaborative then there is an abuse of power. Such is the case in Australia where nonviolent movements press the federal government to apologize on behalf of the nation to the indigenous peoples for two centuries of abuse. Conversely, whenever a chief executive officer (CEO) of a firm seeks the advice of employees, integrative power is being used and employees feel valued as persons.

Such integrative power may also be described as *reciprocal* power. This clearly operates when people seek to influence others and are simultaneously open to being influenced by them, whether such influence consists of ideas, experience, or compassion, for example. Such reciprocal power is then distinguished from the opposite, negative form of power, *unilateral* power. It is at work when a person or a group seeks to influence others but refuses to be influenced by them. This renders dialogue impossible and constitutes bullying.

Returning to May's original distinction between integrative and nutrient types of positive power: while integrative power is *shared with* others, nutrient power is *used for* or *on behalf of* others, for example, the power that parents exercise *for* their children. Nutrient power can, however, turn into the negative forms of paternalistic or seductive power. Then it becomes bullying.

Paternalism occurs when things are done for others which they could readily do themselves. In this way, rather than let people develop naturally and make their own decisions, bullies use emotional mechanisms to establish and maintain control over others. They seek to build a dependency relationship. In the Catholic Church, for example, when high-ranking Church officials in Rome appoint bishops without due consultation with the people of the relevant diocese or country, it is using power paternalistically. This ultimately damages the legitimate development of local churches and constitutes an act of bullying.[10]

When power is used *seductively*, people are not forced to act against their will but their freedom is still significantly and unnecessarily curtailed even though they may be unaware that this is the case. The violated may be convinced insidiously through flattery that it is right and in their best interest to submit to the bully. For example, managers may employ people whom they know cannot easily obtain work elsewhere. Subtly or otherwise they make it known to them that their employment is at a price, that is, total loyalty to the interests of the manager, even if this means going against the wishes of the directors of a company. This is bullying.

* * *

To develop our understanding of power further, we need to recognize that the power to influence others has its source in authority. *Authority* here means legitimacy to exercise power and there are two broad categories of it: position and personal. People with *position* authority have the capacity to influence others because of the *status* they hold in an organization or group. For example, the United States' President has position authority derived from his office as set out in the Constitution. President Richard Nixon (1969–1974) however abused his position authority when he berated members of Congress who sought to expose his cover-up of the Watergate affair. He acted in a bullying manner.

In child sexual abuse cases, approximately one-third of offenders are relatives of the victims, that is, the offenders have used their authority in the family tragically to bully the violated.[11] Social workers, counselors, and ministers of religion who sexually abuse children similarly use their position authority negatively, that is, they abuse their authority.

Corruption is yet another misuse of position authority by officials which constitutes bullying. Corruption is "the misuse of public power for private profit,"[12] and it really is a disease that infects both the public and private sectors of society. It has two major forms: conventional bribery or petty corruption and grand corruption. Examples of *bribery* or *petty corruption* include the instances in the late 1980s, when two members of Parliament in Britain were bribed to raise "appropriate questions" on behalf of a client and, in the 1990s, when some members of the International Olympic Committee involved in choosing venues for the Olympic Games accepted bribes.[13]

Grand corruption occurs when those in high government office deliberately influence government policies for the sake of private gain. This is not an uncommon custom even in the democracies of developed countries.[14] The indirect cost to innocent people though can be enormous. Money that should be available for the common good is diverted into private bank accounts and the costs of goods are increased to enable the ones paying the bribes to recoup the expenses of making them.[15] In developing countries the impact of corruption can be devastating for poor people directly, for example, by their being forced to pay bribes for public services such as health care or transport. This can push them into absolute poverty, an utterly degrading experience.

Returning to our earlier distinction between position and personal authority: while people with *position* authority are able to influence others because of their *status*, people with *personal* authority are able to influence others because of their individual or personal *gifts*. Intimidators may have personal expertise which enables them to identify and exploit the psychological weaknesses of a victim. Some religious cult leaders have shown this, for example, Jim Jones, who was able to "inspire" approximately nine hundred followers to commit suicide in 1978 in Guyana, and David Koresch who was able to demand blind obedience from many members of the Branch Davidian cult in Waco, Texas, in the early 1990s.[16]

Bullying is an act of violence

While it is clear that bullying involves abuses of power and is an act of violence, there is little agreement about how violence should be defined and understood.[17] It is commonly described as the infliction of physical harm to the human body or to human property through the use of either the body or weapons. But such a description is too restrictive: it would confine bullying to the application of physical force. A more preferable definition, therefore, would consider violence as the "exercise of physical or emotional force to injure or abuse someone."[18] *Emotional* violence, for example, can occur with words, gestures, or even silences. Even this preferred definition needs to be expanded, however, to include *cultural* or *structural* violence. "Poverty is the worst form of violence," said Mohandas Gandhi (1869–1948), in which he uses the term "violence" to mean the social, cultural, economic, and political structures which force people against their will to live in poverty. It is in this sense that we can speak of "a culture of violence or bullying." We will analyze this expression more fully in Chapter 3.

Social scientists and philosophers have disagreed for centuries over whether aggression (which is behind violence) is innate, or instinctive, or whether it has to be learned. The philosopher Thomas Hobbes (1588–1679) believed that individuals have no altruistic tendency nor any natural inclination towards mutual help or peaceful life with others: people act like wolves to obtain what they want. Similarly, Friedrich Nietzsche (1844–1900), who profoundly influenced Hitler and his racist policies (and who continues to influence Western thinking), claimed that the inner drive for personal advantage favors violence. Defining *egoism* as the belief that "other beings have to be subordinate by nature, and sacrifice themselves to us," he concluded egoism is essential to the noble soul![19]

The psychoanalyst Sigmund Freud (1856–1939) concluded that aggression is a consequence of the human death drive. When this instinct is turned inwards, the death wish shows itself in self-punishment which in extreme situations leads to suicide. When this instinct is directed outwards, it reveals itself in violent behavior, including bullying: the innate self-destructiveness of individuals is turned against others.

In brief, psychologists generally identify two major conditions that can provoke an individual to be violent:

firstly, frustration resulting from failure to achieve one's desires and, secondly, an attack or a threat of attack on one's life, material well-being, self-image, or self-esteem.[20] *Social psychologists*, who are primarily concerned about the ways in which *individual behavior* is affected by the lives of others, commonly accept that the causes of violence are deeply rooted in human nature *and* culture. Thus violence may be a way to avoid boredom, to raise self-esteem in the presence of others, to express frustration at not getting what one wants, or to achieve status in society.[21] *Social anthropologists*, by contrast, generally do not focus on individual involvement in violent behavior but aim to identify *qualities of cultures* that foster violence (see Chapter 3). Violence and aggression cannot be explained fully with reference to instincts or heredity: cultural and historical factors also shape them.[22]

Five common types of bullies in the workplace

While many different types of bullies may be encountered in a variety of settings, perhaps the types encountered most often are those that occur in the workplace. Of these, there are five common ones: the *persistent critic*, the *skilled manipulator*, the *space invader*, the *benevolent intimidator,* and the *irresponsible abdicator*.

1. The *Persistent Critic*

This bully subjects a victim to constant nitpicking or fault-finding, sarcastic remarks, excessive work demands, passive aggression, or excessive numbers of memos or letters. Notice the impact on the victim in the following close-up: the feeling of being haunted, excessively controlled, and not trusted. (We will look more closely at qualities of the bully and the reactions of the victim in Chapter 3.)

Close-up: bullying by overload of trivia

When the new manager of our section in the hospital assumed office she began to write to me frequently about trivial issues and to request immediate responses. She would choose the most inappropriate times to do this, for example, just before my holidays or on the eve of presenting major reports to local government. I began to feel as though I was under a waterfall and could not escape. I felt I was constantly haunted by the leader; my sleep was affected, my energy for work declined. I just loathed going to work. No sooner had I replied to one letter explaining a point than another would come demanding more information. For a while she used to phone to pressure me with questions but eventually I was able to stop this.

In my annual reports I would explain not only what was happening in our project but also the philosophy and values upon which it was based. The manager, however, would bypass the substance of the reports and question me about irrelevant details. Then I discovered that she had gone to the CEO in an effort to have the project put directly under her control. The CEO, after consultation with my colleagues and me, refused.

At the times when I did speak with the manager, I found myself becoming angry and weary because she would never allow me to discuss the values of the project and how the project was responding to real needs of human deprivation. She would become obstinate and dogmatic about little things the more I invited her to look at the bigger issues affecting the project. She kept saying I should improve my "public relations" with herself and the hospital yet the more I tried the more she would seek to interfere. It became a hopeless situation.

When I tried to communicate my worries to a member of her team, I was rebuffed. The manager had sent instructions to all team members that their role was to support her and not to listen to complaints from the staff. I protested to the manager but I was told that I was disloyal to the organization and would not listen to sound advice. I began to feel like a non-person. No one was concerned about what was happening to me.

Some staff members have submitted themselves and their projects to the manager's direct control for the sake of peace, but they are enraged at having done so. On my part, I believe in my work and inwardly I refuse to be demeaned. I keep looking for the right moment to insist that I be treated as a person and not as a thing which can be ignored. I have begun to own my own authority and, consequently, I feel better in myself. My energy is no longer being drained away by the bullying.

2. The *Skilled Manipulator*

This bully will sulk when they cannot get their way, flatter superiors while gossiping negatively about their subordinates to them, compliment their victims one minute and berate them the next or use lies or half-truths against them. The manipulator is also adept at causing divisions in a group by cultivating favorites and marginalizing others. The following close-up, described by one of the victims, illustrates what happens when bullying by the CEO of an organization goes unchecked: bullying becomes a way of life infecting the whole system. The organization's mission statement in this case proclaimed that "employees are to be treated with respect" and that "leadership would be exercised in a collaborative style"!

Close-up: patronage and bullying

When my CEO took up his position, he said that, in a spirit of open and collaborative leadership, his door was always open to people with complaints or good ideas. But since then he has listened to certain individuals only and downgraded the normal structures of delegation and consultation. Gossip has flourished because he informs only one person about policy (usually his favorite in the team) and never informs the rest of us.

He developed a patronage procedure: if you were subservient to him, flattered him, then there was a chance you could get what you wanted. If he did not like you, then you lived in fear lest suddenly you would be told to leave or be passed over for promotion. A very demoralizing atmosphere developed in which no one could trust anyone.

Board members recognized that some bullying was occurring, but they hesitated to intervene because, they said, this CEO was improving the hospital's financial reserves. Employees who complained to the CEO were branded "dangerous agitators" or "disloyal managers" and were encouraged to leave.[23]

This study highlights two critical points: misuse of power by the bullying CEO and collusion by board members in the intimidation of victims. The CEO had *position* power, that is, he had the authority to direct people's actions after due consultation but he did not use such power appropriately. Instead, he used it to intimidate people into submission: people complied with his directions without comment for fear of losing their jobs.

The CEO also had *personal* gifts of persuasion and financial expertise which he used effectively in relating to board members. They felt flattered by his praise of them or intimidated by the superior knowledge that he claimed to have. Board members who were suspicious of his methods, however, thought that by appeasing him he would cease to bully employees. By not challenging the bully though, these members colluded in his abusive actions. Indirectly, they became bullies themselves by giving implicit permission to the CEO to continue to act unjustly.

Pilate also colluded with the bullying crowd that cried for the death of Jesus. He sought unsuccessfully to dissociate himself from it by a face-saving ritual of washing his hands in public (Matthew 27:24). However, this did not remove the guilt he incurred from conspiring with those who bullied Jesus to death.

Close-up: failure to maintain communication

A parish council consulted widely and over a long period about the idea of building a new church. Other members of the parish community appreciated the way in which the council explained what was proposed, listened sincerely to suggestions, and, finally, they voted in favor of the scheme.

After the project got under way the people in the community were regularly asked for money but they felt that they were not being kept informed about changes that were being made in the plans. Rumors started about mismanagement, misuse of funds, and authoritarianism. The project, instead of uniting the parish, came to divide it, bitterly.

Parishioners finally discovered that the original consultation was merely an effort to manipulate them into financing the building of the new church but without respecting any of their suggestions. When communication stopped, they felt used, angry, and powerless to do anything.

3. The *Space Invader*

This type of bully breaches boundaries whether they be physical, role-related, or emotional. *Physical* invasion may take the form of entering the geographic or intimate territory of another person without just reason or their permission, for example, entering another's office, opening their mail, and getting access to their private files and computer information. One victim described what he felt in such a situation when he discovered that the private notes and research files in his office had been opened and transferred to another office without his knowledge and permission: "I felt personally violated because the room and the files were an extension of myself. My private space had been attacked. Because no one came to my defense, I felt socially as though I had become a non-person, that I had ceased to exist."

A bully breaches *role* boundaries when, for example, they indiscriminately withdraw authority from others or constantly interfere unnecessarily in their victim's work. *Emotional* invasion occurs when abusive language or gestures are used.

4. The *Benevolent Intimidator*

This bully is skilled at hiding abusive activity, as the following close-up illustrates:

 Close-up: "kindness" hides manipulation

With the approval of his superiors, a manager hired several people to be his assistants, claiming that they had the right qualities for the work. He had not advertised their positions nor had he submitted the recruits to an independent assessment. The new employees were grateful to the manager for appointing them. Over time, however, the assistants felt they could not challenge

> the manager's plans because they sensed this would be seen as being disloyal to him, the one who had given them employment when they were in difficult circumstances.

In being dependent on the manager, and so not being free to question his policies and management style, these assistants were subjected to a subtle form of bullying.

5. The *Irresponsible Abdicator*

Recently, there have been several disastrous corporate financial collapses which have caused widespread losses and fear among shareholders, for example, the collapse of HIH Insurance and OneTel in Australia, and Enron and Worldcom in the United States. In the case of the latter two corporations, the retirement and pension funds of millions of people were drastically reduced.

Such corporate collapses have raised the critical issue of good governance. If corporation leaders fail to govern responsibly they act in a bullying manner towards innocent people, at least indirectly. Reflecting on the American collapses, William George, an American expert on corporate governance, believes there is a breakdown in the principles of governance:

> Some boards are just complacent. They fail to challenge management … Some boards don't have the will — or the courage — to challenge a powerful CEO … They let him run roughshod over them, which apparently happened at Enron. Too many CEOs use their boards as a rubber stamp and actively discourage input or challenges from their independent directors.[24]

Hence, not only do many CEOs intimidate or bully their boards but the board members themselves, in refusing to exercise their rightful authority over CEOs, abuse their shareholders: shareholders may subsequently, when crises arise, find themselves ill informed about the performance of corporations in which they have invested. When board members of such corporations abdicate their authority, they are power abusers and therefore bullies.

Other types of bullying in the workplace and beyond

Beyond the five common types of bullying in the workplace, there is a large range of bullying behaviors which occur in a variety of settings ranging from cyberspace to our social lives, to our family and domestic environments,[25] and while ethnic, gender, and religious violence may occur in these settings too, we will delay our consideration of them until Chapter 2. For the meantime, we will consider the following more particular types of bullying:

☑ *Terrorist bullying.* Terrorists deliberately create and exploit "fear through violence or the threat of violence in pursuit of political change."[26] They aim to evoke fear not just in their immediate victims, but *primarily* in the wider community. Such is the case with contemporary international terrorism, for example, the al-Qaeda attacks in the United States in 2001.

Terrorism dramatically illustrates all the components of the functional definition of bullying we explored at the beginning of this chapter: it is a massive abuse of power to dominate people for political or other types of gratification, the fear it creates is persistent and it demeans and degrades people who are defenseless. But what of the inadequacies of the terrorists? They attempt to conceal their lack of self-discipline, especially their lack of perseverance in seeking satisfaction through nonviolent means such as negotiation and dialogue.

☑ In *cyberbullying* the violator uses e-mail or Internet forums to send aggressive mail to victims. Following the terrorist attacks to which we have just referred, the owners of one of Australia's most frequented websites was forced to remove their online discussion board because an unprecedented level of race hate material was being posted on it.[27]

As computers become less expensive, simpler to use, and more readily available, bullies of all kinds are rushing to use the power of modern technology to spread their intimidation of individuals and groups both nationally and internationally.[28] Serial bullies rarely possess good communication skills and the impersonal quality of e-mail permits the intimidator to terrorize indiscriminately.

Computer technology has also provided opportunities for pornography to be far more widely available to consumers than ever before. One American study found that cyberporn (pornography on the Internet) was more graphic, violent, and deviant than pornographic material published before the advent of the Internet and it also found that one-half of nearly six million downloads of computer pornography were related to images of children or adolescents.[29] Not only are the people involved in the production of this material abused but such material demeans the dignity of *all* women and children.

☑ *Groupthink bullying.* Groupthink is a deliberately pejorative expression used to describe others' decline in mental efficiency, reality testing, and moral judgments which becomes obvious when they succumb to subtle bullying group pressures.[30] In submitting to groupthink, people attempt so earnestly to agree with one another that they avoid mentioning alternatives lest divisions emerge in their group. Groupthink can cause a sense of righteous wellbeing in the group's culture that is quite ill-founded. Would-be dissenters are bullied into silence by a fear of punishment by the group or embarrassment. Irving Janis, a social psychologist at Yale University, argues that groupthink caused the Bay of Pigs disaster in Cuba:

President John F. Kennedy's advisers adopted a unanimous position even though privately as individuals they thought differently; conformity grew out of a sense of loyalty to the group.[31]

Close-up: a diocesan senate trapped in groupthink

A bishop called a meeting of his senate to seek advice about the building of a new cathedral. After some preliminary superficial discussion, he said: "My sense is that there is general agreement about going ahead. I presume no one really objects to this work in honor of the Lord." In fact, two members of the senate did have reservations, but felt that in the light of the overall agreement in the group it would cause less trouble not to speak — and they said to themselves, "We depend on the bishop for our promotion."

When news of the building plan was published, there was a bitter outcry from other priests and lay people in the diocese. Questions like the following emerged: "What about faith education programs that are already underfunded? Do we really need a new cathedral when there is a large parish church already in the city center?" All very valid questions.

The bishop's mistake was not to attempt to consult all the people in the diocese who would be concerned about the building of a new cathedral, or at least a representative sample of them. He did not want to "reality test" his plan by submitting it to wider scrutiny for fear that it would be rejected. Instead, he consulted an unrepresentative sample — his senate — who by background and status were too like-minded. The bishop's fear of having his proposal rejected reinforced the senate's desire to conform to his wishes and an atmosphere of groupthink emerged that was so strong that it blocked the senate's ability to listen to would-be dissenting voices.[32]

☑ *Vertical bullying*, the abuse of power by superiors, for example, supervisors or managers. This is sometimes referred to as role bullying. *Horizontal* bullying may also occur between members of one's own peer group.

☑ *Passive bullying* occurs when people are intimidated by having to witness other people being bullied in a more obvious, for example, more physical, way. Hence, bullying incidents at the workplace can have disturbing consequences for colleagues who inadvertently witness them. They become tense themselves, often feel powerless to do anything, and may become fearful that they will be the next target for the rage of the violator. In a study conducted by Cary Cooper of the University of Manchester, practically half of the respondents reported that, over a five year period, they had been involved in passive bullying by witnessing angry scenes in the office or on the shop floor.[33]

In settings which are more social or recreational than the workplace we may encounter the following types of bullying:

☑ *Group bullying*, which occurs when people support a bully either because they are bullies themselves or they fear that if they do not support a ring leader they will become their next victim. Examples of group bullying are football crowds that intimidate supporters of the opposing team. More enduring than such crowds are gangs which develop for the purpose of violent behavior.[34]

☑ *Sport bullying* may include elements of group bullying but also encompass other kinds of bullying which are favored by an emphasis on winning. Spectators may intimidate opposition players or referees who make controversial decisions with racist or other comments, and the players themselves may intimidate members of the opposing team by physical or psychological threats or both. A famous example is the 1932–1933 Bodyline cricket series between Australia and England. The English players persistently (and successfully) sought to intimidate Australian team members through a dangerous style of bowling, a style which has since been outlawed in the game.

☑ *Media bullying.* The media abuse their role in society when journalists invade the privacy of people who have little or no capacity to defend themselves. A CEO of a national organization describes how he feels when he is pressured repeatedly by reporters to reveal confidential information: "I feel constantly hounded by the press. They try to waylay me outside my house and office. I know they are not after the truth but look for a quick, 'news-catchy' or sensational and unfounded story. From experience I know they will twist whatever I say away from the truth so that innocent people will be hurt. I also know that I have no means to correct their reporting. I feel powerless, unless I can evade them."[35]

☑ *Consumer bullying* is illustrated by shoppers who berate and intimidate staff with ill-founded complaints, or patients who constantly verbally abuse nurses.

☑ *Road-rage bullying.* Road rage is the abusive behavior a driver hurls at another with whom he or she is not usually acquainted. An Australian study estimates that about half of all traffic accidents in the country may be due to road rage![36]

☑ *Gender bullying.* This type covers such behaviors as physical, psychological, and sexual bullying between people of opposite gender, whether they all be adults or a mixture of adults and children.

☑ *"Symbolic" bullying* refers to the symbolic nature of the victims whom a bully may choose. A bully may judge victims to represent, for example, a culture which they feel is oppressing them. Eldridge Cleaver, a convicted rapist of white women in the United States in the 1960s, explains the motivation for his crimes: "[The] particular women I had victimized had not been actively involved in oppressing me or other black people. I was taking revenge on them for what the whole system was responsible for."[37]

Finally, in the family and domestic scene, there seems to be an increase in:

☑ *Elder bullying*, which refers to the abuse of elderly people through the willful and persistent deprivation of food or medical treatment, financial exploitation, neglect or physical, emotional, and sexual abuse. Their abusers are generally people in a position of trust, such as family members or other caregivers.

While the prevalence of such abuse is not known accurately, it is assumed generally to be high since populations in Western societies are aging.[38] Reflecting on the Australian situation, Kate Legge, a social commentator and features writer, comments: "The population is aging; people are living longer and remarrying more, often blurring the lines of inheritance; financial affairs are more complex; and dementia clouds the landscape, making its victims vulnerable to pressure and abuse from predators from within their family."[39]

Regardless of setting though, there is always the risk of the following type of bullying:

☑ *Reverse bullying*. It arises when a victim adopts the bullying behavior of their former oppressor once the oppression ceases. Either the former violator or other people may become victims of the former victim. Victims and violators, beware!

Summary

1. Power is the ability to influence others in a negative *or* positive sense. It is positive when it is used with the aim of empowering others. Such power includes integrative (or reciprocal) and nutrient types. Power is negative when it is used to dominate and control others unduly. Types of negative power include those which are unilateral, paternalistic, or seductive.

2. Bullying, a form of violence, is the use of power to dominate, demean, and humiliate people who consequently lose self-confidence and self-esteem.

3. Bullying is a widespread social disease found in all forms of employment, cultures, and organizations, including the churches.

4. The roots of bullying are not only in instincts and heredity but also in cultures. We will explore this theme in Chapter 3.

Questions

1. Have you ever been bullied? What did it feel like? What did you do about it? If you did nothing, what could you have done instead?

2. Read Luke 4:28-30 in which the people of Jesus' own hometown attempt to intimidate him. Why were they feeling so strongly towards Jesus? What do you think Jesus was feeling?

3. Is anyone being bullied in your home or workplace? What qualities do you notice in the bully? What can you do to help the victim?

Chapter 2

Bullies and Victims

It is not power that corrupts but fear.
Fear of losing power corrupts those who wield it
and fear of the scourge of power
corrupts those who are subject to it.

Aung San Suu Kyi[1]

This chapter explores:

☛ the characteristics of a bully
☛ sex differences in bullying
☛ the relationships between prejudice,
discrimination, and bullying
☛ the impact of bullying on victims
☛ the similarity between the consequences of
bullying and post-traumatic stress disorder
(PTSD)

and concludes with biblical reflections.

The characteristics of a bully

Among the typical features of bullies are personal inadequacies, including an inability to express emotion, an
abnormally high potential for sadism, and a perverted desire
for immortality. Often too they are narcissistic and feel the
need to control others.

Personal inadequacies

Bullies are people who feel inadequate and deeply lonely
in themselves; they are overly sensitive to criticism and

fear losing face. To avoid dealing with whatever defi-
ciencies they may have, they divert others' attention from
them by bullying people less powerful than themselves.
According to psychologist Melanie Klein, the bully feels
an inner rage over their own sense of inadequacy and
projects it onto some other object or person, the victim.
The victim they abuse to contain their inner rage becomes
a "bad object" to them, an object to be destroyed through
harassing behavior.[2]

As a consequence of projecting their own inner inadequacies onto others, bullies are more likely to perceive
unfriendly intentions in others, even though there may be
no objective reasons for perceiving such intentions.[3] The
last thing a bully wants is to be found to have inadequacies
and to have his or her favorite seemingly positive self-
image deflated. Thus, the more attention they can direct
to the supposed failings of the victim, the better they feel
in themselves.

Close-up: a pastor as a bully

Luke, a priest in a Catholic parish, has been having
difficulties in relating to Mary, the recently appointed,
female pastoral assistant. Unlike Luke, Mary is highly
educated theologically and committed to the collaborative principles of the Second Vatican Council. Luke
frequently criticizes her at parish council meetings
whether or not she says anything, reminding her that
experience, not theoretical knowledge, counts more
in the pastoral ministry.

In this close-up, Luke reflects the paranoid thinking of
bullies: they act out of fear of losing power, even when the
victims are not attempting to take it.

Bullies are often skilled at concealing the nature of their
actions from others. Sometimes they flatter people who

might challenge them, especially if they perceive them to have more power. Bullies may also seduce their victims, attempting to create dependency relationships by offering lavish gifts or through other apparently generous actions. The recipients of such gifts feel obliged then to behave in a submissive way towards the bully.

Inability to express emotion

A common personal inadequacy among bullies is the inability to express emotion. As children, they may never have been shown how to express emotion freely or taught interpersonal skills that would allow them to create loving and positive relationships. In their original families, often they did not experience an atmosphere of supportive love, that is, they rarely felt valued or that they had any worthwhile sense of achievement.[4] For them, aggressive behavior became the expected way of interacting; they may have seen others acting violently at home or they may have been subjected to it themselves as a "normal" way of interacting.

If children have been treated harshly and are deeply affected by it, they transfer such experience into their adult years. Subconsciously, they seek opportunities to relive the experience so that they might redress the balance but in such instances, rather than being the victim, they enact the role of aggressor.[5]

In this way, it is quite likely that school bullies become adult bullies, though the form of intimidation they hand out may alter. Playground bullying may well develop into sexual harassment, gang attacks, date violence, assault, marital violence, child abuse, workplace harassment, or elder abuse. The common factor in all of these forms of bullying behavior is the combination of power and aggression, a behavioral pattern that is learned early and continues unless it is corrected.[6]

From his research into abusive males, Donald Dutton, a professor of psychology at the University of British Columbia, concludes that three types of experience in childhood contribute simultaneously to the development of adult bullies: firstly, being made to feel insecure in relationships which have a strong emotional component by, for example, being made to feel deserted by a parent or caretaker; secondly, being involved in incidents when they were made to feel ashamed and hence inadequate as a person by, for example, a parent; and thirdly, being made the victim of passive bullying by, for example, having seen an adult, usually a parent, actually being overtly abusive to someone else.[7]

Narcissism and a need to control others

Bullies rarely have empathy for the people they harass. They are so caught up in their own narcissistic fear of losing power that they are oblivious to the effect they have on their victims. As psychoanalyst Neville Symington writes, the narcissism of a bully is "a particular state of mind where the individual has taken his own ego as love object. Such a situation precludes compassion for others ... The narcissistic person is unable to see something from the other person's point of view because the other does not exist emotionally."[8] All of this makes it difficult to reason with bullies. They are simply blocked from hearing the logic of arguments used in favor of their victims so that when positive information is provided in support of them, bullies will immediately attack their victims from another angle. If the victims themselves become angry with the bullies, their anger merely fuels their own inner rage.

Bullies are consumed with the desire to control the lives of others but not because they are concerned for their welfare: they are concerned only with what can serve their own narcissistic desires. Earnestly, but unsuccessfully, they seek personal recognition, but when they fail to achieve it honorably, they seek it through the abuse of power, and the more they fail to achieve recognition even dishonorably, the more they abuse others.[9]

Bullies may speak in a seemingly eloquent way about how people should act according to noble principles, but these principles do not guide their own behavior. Instead, they view relationships in terms of domination and submission, demanding that others conform to their wishes. Typically, they lack spontaneity and are unable to relax; they present themselves as hard working but their behavior is rigid, anxiety-ridden, and repetitive, and they lack imagination. Bullies are prone to overreaction and exaggerated gestures of generosity to people who are prepared to submit to their views. Those who do not do so are likely to become targets of revenge.

Potential for sadism

Bullies have an abnormally high potential for being sadistic. As the psychoanalyst Erich Fromm writes: "The pleasure in complete domination over another person ... is the very essence of the sadistic drive. Another way of formulating the same thought is to say that the aim of sadism is to transform a man [*sic*] into a thing, something animate into something inanimate, since by complete and absolute control the living loses one essential quality of life — freedom."[10]

Forcing someone to experience pain or humiliation without their being able to defend themselves is one of the symptoms of being under the absolute control of a sadist, but we should note that Fromm distinguishes the sadist from the *destroyer*. The destroyer desires to do away with a person, to eliminate them, to destroy life itself, but "the sadist wants the sensation of controlling and choking life ... Living beings are transformed into living, quivering, pulsating objects of control."[11]

Desire for immortality

Ernest Becker, social theorist and Pulitzer Prize winner, believes that human beings cannot accept the reality of death and that violence, particularly murder and bullying, may give the perpetrator a feeling of immortality and invulnerability. As the Nazi regime was collapsing, its leaders tried to affirm their sense of immortality by horrible acts of bullying and killing. Becker writes: "Sadism naturally absorbs the fear of death ... because by actively manipulating and hating we keep our organism absorbed in the outside world; this keeps self-reflection and fear of death in a state of low tension. We feel we are masters over life and death when we hold the fate of others in our hands."[12] His comments may also apply to the waves of killing and destruction perpetrated by the Indonesian military and pro-Indonesian militia in East Timor in 1999, following the East Timorese people's decision to seek independence from Indonesia.

A less disturbing view than Becker's is that bullying gives people a sense of personal identity when they feel inadequate in the presence of others. At times, bullies may have a very high opinion of themselves, but it is a fragile self-image which they fear could easily be deflated by others. Above all, they fear being shamed in public.[13]

Sex differences in bullying

In Britain, men are more likely than women to be convicted of a violent offence: approximately 90 percent of child molesters, for example, are males.[14] Cultural factors foster the bullying aggressiveness of men: in a variety of ways,

Western society approves of men who dominate relationships at the expense of women (an issue that will be examined further in Chapter 3). Girls are expected to be submissive; and boys are expected to act out society's image of masculinity which includes recklessness and toughness.

The definition of manhood in the United States has been succinctly summarized by psychologist Robert Brannon. According to his analysis, men are expected to live out the following four slogans:[15]

- *no sissy stuff,* that is: repudiate anything that is feminine

- *be a big wheel:* measure your manhood by your power, success, and wealth

- *be a sturdy oak:* show no emotions

- *give 'em hell:* be daring and aggressive.

In view of such a cultural exaltation of male toughness, with its emphasis on disparaging feminine qualities, it is little wonder that the rates of abuse by men against women, gay men, and lesbians are high.[16] Barbara Perry, a professor of criminal justice at Northern Arizona University, argues from research into the extent of hate crimes in the United States that "anti-gay violence tends to be the most brutal of all such victimizations."[17]

Assessing the evidence in Australia, social commentator Stephen Tomsen concludes that there "is growing evidence that members of this minority group (gay men and lesbians) experience disproportionately high levels of violence, much of it in the form of hate crime."[18] Also, a survey of Australian research has found that between eight and 50 percent of gay men and lesbians report having been the victims of physical assault because of their sexual orientation.[19]

As children, *girls* bully others by spreading derogatory rumors about them, encouraging companions to dislike them, and threatening to cease being a friend if the victim refuses to submit. As adults, this subtle and hidden form of bullying remains: since women tend to depend more than men on maintaining good relationships with others, a bully among females may intimidate a victim by threatening to exclude her socially.[20] Even though bullying among females may be indirect more than is the case among males, it is no less painful. A Finnish study, for example, found the victims of bullying among females to be more depressed than the victims of bullies among males.[21]

Prejudice, discrimination, and bullying

Prejudice is the holding of preconceived opinions either against, or in favor of, someone or some social, cultural, or racial group, but the term is probably most often used in the negative sense — the sense that we will use it here — to refer to an attitude of antipathy or active hostility towards others. Bullies feed on such negativity to maintain their addiction to controlling and subjugating victims, and their victims in turn suffer *discrimination*. Again, this is a term which may be used negatively or positively but we will use it here in the negative sense in which it is most frequently used.

Since prejudice lies behind bullying, we will explore further what prejudice means and the various types of prejudice and discrimination. Prejudice consists of two elements: a stereotype and a feeling. A *stereotype* is a preformed image of things or people; it is a shorthand but faulty method of handling a complex world. By placing people in preformed categories by, for example, assuming that groups of people are inferior because they differ from us in their skin color, customs, or language, we can feel that we are controlling threats to our sense of order, meaning, or cultural purity. Because every culture has many stereotypes of people from other cultures, the members of any one culture tend to be prejudiced towards the members of other cultures.

Prejudices are not just made up of stereotypes though: they are often motivated by strong, powerful *feelings* which lead a prejudiced person to see only what he or she expects to see, or even to see things that are not there at all. For example, a white Australian who sees a well-dressed white man running down a street in the heart of Sydney might interpret such an event as a man trying to catch a bus. However, if the person running were to be a black male youth, the white Australian, given the widespread negative racial stereotypes in Australian culture about Aboriginal peoples, might interpret the event as a mugger escaping from the scene of a crime. That is what people who think this way say they *see*.

Since the terrorist attacks on the United States, many Muslims have been assaulted on the prejudiced assumption that *all* Muslims are terrorists. It is not a matter of logical thought or deduction but a question of perception based on a preformed stereotype. This type of prejudice by its nature sets up a hostile and potentially bullying relationship with other people.

Example: Jesus is bullied: prejudice in action

Jesus on one occasion spoke of how the people perceived John the Baptist and himself: "For John came neither eating nor drinking, and they say: 'He has a demon' the Son of Man came eating and drinking, and they say, 'Look, a glutton and a drunkard, a friend of tax collectors and sinners!'" (Matt 11:18-19)

No matter what Jesus did, his enemies would see only evil in him and his disciples.

One of the most tragic effects of prejudice is when members of a minority group *believe* the prejudices that the dominant group holds against them. When they accept and live out the stereotypes of inferiority held by the dominant society, it is extremely difficult to help them to recognize their human potential and dignity. African Americans in the southern states of the United States of America, for example, had so interiorized the dominant society's prejudice that they were inferior that when Martin Luther King Jr. (1929–1968) attempted to foster support among them for his civil rights movement, he found it extremely difficult. Likewise in Australia among the Aboriginal peoples: since 1788, they have passed through every kind of negative experience at the hands of the dominant immigrant society except total extermination. The ridiculing of their cultural heritages and their own interiorization of the dominant society's prejudices against them have often led to tragic consequences, both collectively and individually. Hence, Ruth Fink reports that some Aboriginal people in Australia show "an aggressive assertion of low-status; it seems to say 'Look at me — I'm colored and I'm dirty, drunken, lazy and irresponsible, like they say — that's my privilege, because I'm colored — I can do as I like, because that's what they expect of me anyway.' "[22]

Types of prejudice

Prejudice may be based on any one or more personal characteristics including cultural (or ethnic) and racial membership, sex, and religion.

1. Cultural (or ethnic) and racial prejudice

People of every culture or nation tend to think that their way of life is the right one and that other ways of acting are stupid, crude, uncivilized, unreasonable, evil, or super-stitious. Technically, such prejudice is called *ethnocentrism* and it can develop into ethnic discrimination. The psychologist Gordon Allport describes this as "an antipathy based upon a faulty and inflexible generali-zation. It may be felt or expressed. It may be directed towards a group as a whole, or towards an individual because he [or she] is a member of that group."[23] Notice the reference to "faulty and inflexible generalization," that is, to the two aspects of prejudice: the meaning and feeling dimensions.

Ethnic prejudice can readily degenerate into *racial* prejudice, which is the assumption that races vary in intelligence, cultural, and moral qualities simply because of the genetic make-up of their members. When oppressors go to the extreme of branding people of other races *nonhuman*, they consider them merely to be animals to be discriminated against, even killed with impunity. Such was the case for Jews under Hitler.

2. Sexual prejudice

The prejudice of sexism is the assumption that a person is inferior as a human being because they belong to one sex and hence not to the other.[24] Sexism assumes, for example, that members of a particular sex are objects to be used freely for pleasure or for the preservation of the dominant position of the members of one sex. Anti-female prejudice is extremely common in most cultures of the world; women are falsely considered to be intellectually and emotionally inferior and childlike when compared with men. Women are regarded as being incapable of participating equally with men in making decisions that concern society or even themselves.

Two examples from my own experience illustrate how Western society has falsely taken the inferiority of women for granted. Prejudices exist deep in our collective un-conscious, influencing our feelings in negative and harmful ways in which we may be unaware.

 Examples

In the mid 1970s, after lecturing to a group of people gathered from various nations, I sat down expecting considerable praise to come my way for all the preparation I had done on my lecture. One woman, however, immediately stood up and vigorously attacked me: "You are a sexist! You used the word 'man' thirty times!"

The woman was right. I had spoken in a highly insensitive way, sending a strong message to the audience that women were of no importance.

On another occasion, I was on a plane when it leveled off and the captain spoke. Because the captain's voice was that of a woman, I was im-mediately fearful for the safety of the plane.

The stereotype in Western culture falsely says "Women are not mechanical; they cannot fly planes!" I had unconsciously accepted my culture's assump-tion of women's inferiority.

3. Religious prejudice

Once a religious group believes it has the monopoly on truth concerning what it means to live in a right rela-tionship with God, that is, that it believes it has nothing to learn from any other religion on the subject, then there is religious prejudice. For centuries, Catholic Christians looked on Protestant Christians as thorough heretics, lost to Christ, and Protestants in their turn thought the same of Catholics. This prejudice is less evident today, except in places such as Northern Ireland, but in some parts of the world deep-seated prejudices between Christians and Muslims have now come to the surface.

Discrimination: some contemporary types

The types of discrimination victims suffer correspond with the types of prejudice their oppressors have. Hence, we can distinguish ethnic and racial, sexual and religious types of discrimination.

1. Ethnic and racial discrimination

Not infrequently, members of minority ethnic groups feel that the dominant group, police, and courts are prejudiced against them.

Examples

Social scientist Ross Hampton in New Zealand comments that: "The judicial system labels a large proportion of Maori males as having a criminal character, and this would lead the public and police to give any Maori male the label of 'criminal' even *before* he acquires an official record. This would help to explain also the increased likelihood of prosecution of Maori youths at the first offence."[25]

In Australia, journalist Paola Totaro notes another expression of ethnic discrimination: "Crime involving ethnic minorities is regarded as a problem for leaders of a community to solve. Yet if it is a crime involving the white majority, it's a general community problem."[26]

In Britain, social science research confirms the existence of racism among police:[27] blacks are five times more likely than whites to be stopped by police, more likely to be charged, more likely to be denied bail, more likely to suffer injury in police cells, and more likely to be jailed if convicted. Although racial prejudice is not the only factor contributing to the severer treatment of people with black skin compared to those having skin of another color, it is now admitted to be a significant influence.[28]

In recent years, open racism in Western societies has re-emerged. It is expressed particularly in hate movements and in crimes directed against foreign workers, asylum seekers, poor immigrants, and minorities made up of members of various nationalities (see Chapter 3 for a fuller description). Such racism is encouraged by far right political parties and the crimes it fosters are often committed by young, unemployed people.[29]

2. Sexual discrimination

Sexual discrimination, as already noted, commonly springs from deep anti-female prejudice. Despite a rise in the consciousness of the prevalence of such discrimination in Western society, women are still discriminated against, especially in relation to employment. In the health service in Britain, for example, women still suffer from inequality of job opportunity and poor pay, and they occupy a dispropor-tionately large number of low status positions.[30] Similarly in Australia, women health specialists are confined to certain areas considered to be "women's work," areas of medicine considered to be of relatively low status, including gynecology, pediatrics, and plastic surgery.[31] Finally, in the 1990s, almost 60 percent of undergraduates in Australian universities were female, yet women constituted only 5 percent of the professors and associate professors on their teaching and research staffs.[32]

3. Discrimination within religious settings

The churches have been adversely affected for centuries by patriarchy which, in recent decades, has come to be understood as not just male rule but male-instigated bullying of women. The Christian Scriptures have been misused to support patriarchy, and the churches have too readily and uncritically accepted the male-centered cultures in which they exist. In the Church of England, Monica Furlong wrote feelingly on the discrimination she found there,[33] and other writers within the Catholic Church have described two sorts of abuse which patriarchy has helped to foster, namely, clericalism and the use of sexist language.

Clericalism is the belief and practice that only clergy should be involved in the proclamation of the word of God and in ecclesiastical administration and that lay people, especially women, should be submissive, dependent recipients of their labors.[34] The Scripture scholar Carolyn Osiek comments on the devastating impact of clericalism on the self-image of women in the Church: "For women in the churches, even in professional church ministry, the attitude takes the form of the unconscious assumption that anyone in a clerical collar can do it better. How many women parishioners still bypass the lay minister of Communion in favor of the priest?"[35]

For centuries, the prayer language of the Church has been male-oriented or sexist, giving the impression that women do not exist, that they are non-persons. The message seems to have been: God comes to save *men* alone. Use of the word "man" or "men" in communal prayer hence has been felt to exclude females and to connote patriarchal domination. Although the past few decades have seen a general increase in awareness of the problems promoted by using such male-oriented language, there has been little progress in finding ways to avoid its use in common prayer — and maybe even, under Rome's instructions, there has been a regression towards favoring its use.[36]

The impact of bullying on victims

Victims' lives change in various ways in response to bullying. Some people feel forced to change jobs and even to relocate to a different part of their country to escape a bully. Some seek escape in drug and alcohol abuse or experience marital and other relationship problems or suffer psychiatric disturbances. Some even commit suicide. Many victims, though, ultimately resign themselves to enduring the domineering behavior of a bully simply because they cannot find a way to escape it.[37] The factors which contribute to such tragic outcomes include the uncovering of victims' vulnerabilities, the undermining of their self-esteem, their marginalization, a feeling of having their trust in significant others betrayed, being blamed for the abuse themselves, and shame over its mere existence. Let us now consider these a little more closely.

The uncovering of victims' vulnerabilities

Bullies enviously target people who are competent, conscientious, particularly popular with others, or noted for their honesty and integrity. They identify and exploit the weaknesses of such people, for example, their shyness, membership of a minority group such as a race or a particular sex, differences in their educational background, speech or accent, or even their status as a single parent. Bullies' ability to sense the vulnerabilities or fears of others is uncanny and they take advantage of them.[38] As Peter Randall, a British authority on adult bullying, comments: "It is axiomatic that wherever there is power it is likely to be abused, and wherever there is vulnerability there is likely to be exploitation."[39] Andrew Harrison, a British parachute regiment officer trapped by rebels in Sierra Leone in mid 2000, was aware of this trick of his captors as he recorded: "I was trying to remain stoical because if you showed fear it gave the rebels power."[40]

The undermining of victims' self-esteem

A victim described her experience of being bullied by the manager at her workplace: "I felt terrorized. Even the sight of him made me feel paralyzed, impotent. On seeing a memo from him, even by e-mail, I would go into a panic. I kept getting letters from him demanding that I do this or that and insisting that he had the authority on his side. I felt paralyzed."[41]

By being made to feel impotent and fearful, this woman's self-confidence and self-esteem were undermined, but bullies may undermine victims' self-worth in other ways too. For example, they may cause victims to suffer shock that they have been singled out for attack, or depression, sleep disorders, poor concentration, chest pains, or even rage. Further, victims may feel guilty, believing that they are responsible for their distress, something that particularly pleases the violator. Yet, if the victim attempts to defend themselves, the bully reacts with further abuse; victims who complain are commonly branded as troublemakers. The last thing a bully wants is to be found out and to have his or her intolerable behavior revealed by a whistleblower. Hence, the more attention directed to the victim's supposed failings, the better for the violator.

Robyn Mann, a researcher in business communications in Australia, has shown that bullies in the workplace use subtle techniques of intimidation, in contrast to the loud aggressiveness commonly associated with more obviously physical forms of bullying. Psychological abuse, she concludes, "usually manifests through such acts as quiet comment and nonverbal communication, often on a one-to-one basis, as well as deliberate exclusion, derogatory rumors and setting up for failure."[42]

Sometimes, a bully will deliberately reassure a victim of his or her esteem for them, then suddenly intimidate them. For example, one particular form of intimidation used by

Stalin was to assure his victims they were safe, only to arrest them or members of their family shortly afterwards. Some victims would be arrested, tortured, and given severe prison sentences, only to be released a few months or years later and granted high office. By such methods, Stalin, an archbully, wanted to show people his absolute power and control: victims never knew with any certainty whether or not they were in favor with him.[43]

Marginalization

> The ultimate injustice is for a person or group to be actively treated or passively abandoned as if they were non-members of the human race.[44]

Often, a victim is ostracized even by close friends or work colleagues, who fear that they themselves will become victims. To avoid this from happening though they may turn into sycophants of the bully. They then collude in the harassment of the victim. Bystanders may even encourage victims somehow to placate a bully but this will inevitably feed a bully's yearning for more power over their victim. This was the case with Neville Chamberlain (1869–1940), the British Prime Minister who tried to appease Hitler by giving way to his demands in relation to Czechoslovakia in 1938. Ultimately, his action led to Hitler's push to gain more territory and consequently to World War II.

Victims and their supporters usually find it useless to argue rationally with a bully because their intimidation is not a rational action. The bully will find ways to trap the victim into a deeper sense of powerlessness and frighten off supporters from becoming involved.

The following close-up illustrates the various stages that bullying may pass through up to the end stage of the marginalization (or "amputation") of the victim as well as the subtle verbal and nonverbal ways bullies act when seeking control.

Close-up: research ignored

For several months, a corporate executive had researched how best his department could extend its services into another area of his city. He prepared a report which included a recommended plan of action and was sent to other members of the corporation's executive, but the moment he presented it to the group in person, he felt a coldness and impatience. Without his knowledge, the CEO and other executives had a different plan which they were intent on implementing, regardless of his research-based recommendations.

The CEO said to the researcher: "Your plan is good, but it is not as good as ours." He and others tried to argue with him about the value of their plan (the "rational" stage) but it became obvious that the group had not studied the researcher's plan before the meeting.

After the CEO called for a coffee break, several executives went to him and said: "Look, you are a good friend (the 'emotional seduction' stage). Why can't you see things our way like you have always done?" The researcher stood his ground, asking that his plan be seriously considered, but this provoked an abusive response: "You are stubborn! You are impossible to work with!" (the "formal bullying stage").

Back at the conference table, the meeting resumed. The researcher felt very strange then because it was as though he no longer existed: no eyes turned to him, no questions on other matters were directed to him (the "amputation" or "marginalization" stage).

Later, he left his job and the CEO's plan failed: none of the other executives challenged its weaknesses because they feared receiving the same treatment that the researcher had been given.[45]

Notice in this close-up how the victim's colleagues collude with the CEO. The victim is marginalized by all the members of the executive: socially, he becomes a non-person. This was an extremely painful experience for him, especially since he was committed to his work. He further described his feelings of exclusion in this way: "It was a strange and horrible experience to remain in the same room as the others once my views were overlooked. It was as though I no longer existed in the room. People would look at me but without any expression of recognition on their faces. If I had departed they would not have noticed."

The betrayal of trust

Victims experience a betrayal of the trust they place in significant other persons when they appear to promote their welfare yet bully them or fail to prevent their being bullied by third parties. For example, in the case of child sexual abuse, children may feel a betrayal of the trust they have in their parents or in some government or other official agency, for example, the police, or the clergy. Again, employees may feel betrayed by their workplace manager, or priests by their bishop, when such leaders persistently refuse to listen to constructive suggestions, yet at the same time openly proclaim that they are committed to a culture of dialogue and openness. On a broader scale, vulnerable citizens such as disturbed people, gay and lesbian groups, and ethnic and racial minorities, feel betrayed by society in general when they are refused protection.

The blaming of victims for their abuse

Victims of bullying are constantly in danger of not being believed by those to whom they report their distress or of being ignored or even blamed for the problem. Rape victims, for example, usually fear that they will not be believed or will be blamed for being the cause of the abuse.

Psychologists Alexander McFarlane and Bessel Van der Kolk write: "Society's reactions to traumatized people … are primarily the results of conservative impulses in the service of maintaining the belief that the world is essentially good, that 'good' people are in charge of their lives, and that bad things only happen to 'bad' people … Victims are the members of society whose problems represent the memory of suffering, rage, and pain in a world that longs to forget."[46]

Shame that abuse exists

Shame is the sense that we have somehow failed as a person. Victims of bullying can feel shame because they and others see that they are vulnerable in the presence of bullies. *They* are the ones chosen to be the targets of abuse, not other people. This is felt to be a shaming and deeply humiliating experience. Because of this, victims will often try to hide the existence of the abuse they suffer in order to avoid public shame. Openly admitting the existence of domestic violence, for example, can be rendered difficult or impossible "by shame about not being loved by one's spouse, about being unable to protect oneself and one's children, about failing to bring security and happiness to one's family, and about acknowledging one's physical and financial powerlessness."[47]

The similarity between suffering from bullying and post-traumatic stress disorder

Stress describes a state of acute unease which takes hold of a person when they struggle to cope with overpowering pressures; their mental and physical states are upset, especially their emotions. *Post-Traumatic Stress Disorder* (PTSD) is a technical name given to the cluster of stress reactions that a person may suffer following the first-hand experience of a catastrophe such as being raped or violently assaulted, being caught in the midst of a terrorist attack, or being involved in a severe automobile or rail accident. Such experiences destroy their sense of invulnerability to being hurt. The variety of stress reactions that sufferers of PTSD report include any one or more of the following: heightened physiological arousal, flashbacks, chronic sleep disturbance, nightmares, feelings of despair and depression.[48]

Sometimes, the victims of bullying experience similar stressful reactions to those of the sufferers of PTSD. When they are being bullied, victims feel helpless in the face of overwhelming forces and are psychologically traumatized. Their feelings of control, connection, trust, and meaning can be severely weakened or destroyed.[49] Paul McCarthy, an Australian researcher in the area of workplace bullying, says that 75 percent of people who experience long-term bullying display symptoms of PTSD and are unable to return to work indefinitely.[50]

Biblical reflections

There are many examples of bullying in both the Old and New Testaments, but here we will recall only a few experiences of the victims. In fact, some of the most poignant and, in a sense, beautiful passages in the Bible are the cries of those who have been violated. The lamentation psalms are filled with the incidents of people whose lives have been crushed by others. Their sense of self-worth has been undermined and they are on the verge of despair. Ponder these words of the psalmist (Psalm 41:6-7), who even in grave illness is being terrorized by people and feels the anguish of abandonment by once-trusted friends:

> And when they come to see me,
> they utter empty words,
> while their hearts gather mischief;
> when they go out,

they tell it abroad.
All who hate me whisper together about me.

What particularly pains the psalmist is the fact that an apparently close friend is colluding with the bullies:

Even my bosom friend in whom I trusted,
who ate of my bread,
has lifted heel against me (v. 9).

In a later psalm, Psalm 142, the psalmist describes a similar experience of intimidation:

In the path where I walk they have hidden a trap for me.
Look on my right hand and see —
there is no one who takes notice of me;
no refuge remains to me;
no one cares for me…
I am brought very low (vv. 3, 4, 6).

In the next psalm, Psalm 143, the impact of the bullying is also dramatically depicted. The psalmist has been brought to the verge of despair by the malicious plots of his tormentors. Socially, he has ceased to exist — he has been marginalized — and he is consumed with the fear of what will happen to him next at the hands of his violators:

For the enemy has pursued me,
crushing my life to the ground,
making me sit in darkness like those long dead.
Therefore my spirit faints within me;
my heart within me is appalled (vv. 3, 4).

The prophet Jeremiah, in a pathos-filled complaint to God, describes the depth of inner pain caused by the assailants surrounding him, including former friends:

I have become a laughing-stock all day long;
everyone mocks me…
For the word of the Lord has become for me

a reproach and derision all day long...
I hear many whispering...
All my close friends are watching for me to stumble
(Jer 20:7, 8, 10).

Then there is the most dramatic of all laments: the cry of Jesus on the Cross: "My God, my God, why have you forsaken me?" (Mark 15:34). Passers-by add to the abuse of his executioners by jeering at him (v. 29) and some of those who remain loyal to him watch at a distance (v. 40). Jesus is overwhelmed by a feeling of abandonment, even of abandonment by his Father.

However, in all these biblical laments, a childlike trust in God remains in the hearts of the violated. Jesus, for example, in his cry to his Father, is quoting from Psalm 22 which ends with a proclamation of *trust* in God:

For he [God] did not despise or abhor
the affliction of the afflicted;
he did not hide his face from me,
but heard when I cried to him (v. 24).

Summary

1. Bullies are people with personal inadequacies. They project their own fears onto others in order to control them. Frequently, their domination of others is legitimated by their culture(s). Bullies may be male or female.

2. Prejudices, in the negative sense of the term, are unfavorable feelings towards other persons or things which are not based on first-hand experience. They are *prejudgments*: judgments made before allowing ourselves to be open to experiencing first-hand how other persons or things really are. The varieties of prejudice are expressed in corresponding forms of discrimination. Bullies' prejudices and acts of discrimination maintain their addiction to power.

3. Victims can be devastated by bullying. They may suffer from self-doubt, fear, depression, rage, loss of employment, financial ruin, or marriage breakdown — even suicide.

4. The Scriptures give voice to the plight of victims in the psalms but especially in the accounts of Jesus' life and death.

Questions

1. Which minority groups in your suburb or town are discriminated against with respect to employment or educational opportunities, housing, or freedom of religious expression? What can you do personally to help overcome such discrimination?

2. Read the Letter of St. Paul to the Galatians 3:27-8. What is St. Paul speaking about?

3. As you watch television this week, take a note of the stereotypes about women and men that you see or hear being used.

Chapter 3

Cultures of Bullying

*It is necessary to go straight to the heart of society
in order to identify the cultural resources
in which the authors of violence
find inspiration for their acts…*
Elizabeth Picard[1]

This chapter explores:

☞ the meaning of culture

☞ cultural causes of bullying which undergird
the personal inadequacies of bullies

☞ three models of culture which legitimise
different forms of bullying.

Like most studies of bullying, our attention so far has been
limited mainly to the psychological inadequacies of the
perpetrator and to the effects of bullying on the victim. But
we must move beyond these important aspects to an even
more basic aspect, namely, the environment or cultural
context in which bullying occurs. By doing this, we will
better understand the dynamics of bullying.

The influence of culture on bullying is so powerful that
we can rightly speak at times of *cultures* of bullying. These
are cultures that allow, even encourage, people to bully
others. We have touched on this aspect already when we

were reflecting on how *stereotypes* are deeply embedded in cultures but now we will consider the more hidden *potential* for bullying which lies within cultures. I argue that a culture of bullying or abuse is a collection of traditions, conventions, and language that can be used within a group to legitimize mistreatment of its members or of outsiders and, further, that unless such cultures are examined and modified, intimidation of the powerless will continue.

Two personal incidents illustrate how a bullying mentality can become incorporated in a culture.

 Examples

1. When I was carrying out research in Fijian villages in the mid 1960s, prior to Fiji's independence from the British, I was startled and shocked to hear adult Fijian men describe the fear they felt whenever they had to visit government departments staffed by British officials. One of the men expressed what they all felt: "I would approach the building, my knees becoming weaker and weaker, my stomach filled with fear. When I spoke to an official I would almost lose my voice."

2. Later, during my work in Papua, New Guinea, prior to its independence from Australia, I noticed that whenever a warrior or strong local man had to speak with a white government official, he would keep at a distance, bend his body as though in the presence of some medieval king, and wait patiently until the official gruffly called him.

These two examples clearly demonstrated for me the bullying power of cultures. The culture of colonialism, it seemed, was the same in both countries: it evoked fear and dependency in the local people and therefore could be termed a culture of bullying. The officials however may have been unconscious of the impact of their actions on the people — they were, after all, simply acting in accordance with the value system of their own culture. Let us then move to a deeper understanding of the word "culture."

Defining "culture"

The traditions and customs which help make up a culture are often silent in the sense that they frequently impact on people's values, feelings, and behavior without their being aware of them. Even people who believe that they act rationally and are motivated by principles of efficiency may be unconsciously guided by the rigid and pervasive inner dynamics of culture. In this way, what some people call the "silent language," that is, culture, guides "*what* people do" and also "what people *feel*, whether consciously or unconsciously, about what they do."[2] Such guidance is evident in the following definition of culture:

- a pattern of shared meanings and values,

- embodied in a network of *symbols, myths,* and rituals,

- created by a particular group as it struggles to adjust to life's challenges,

- educating its members about what is considered to be the *orderly* and correct way to feel, think, and behave.

Symbols and myths form the very heart of a culture. *Symbols* convey meanings that evoke good or bad feelings. The sight of a police car after I drive through a red light, for example, causes feelings of fear within me. *Myths*, contrary to popular thinking, are not fairy tales;

they are the narrative symbols or stories which bind people of a culture together, most often unconsciously at the deepest level of their collective being. They are the "emotional glue" of a culture. Without them, we do not know the meanings of things, what to do with them, or how to relate to them. A myth claims to reveal, in an imaginative way, a fundamental truth about the world and human life, a truth which is regarded as authoritative by those who accept it.

 Example

The creation mythology of the white people of New Zealand society describes how the country was colonized by hardy, adaptable, democracy-seeking, and creative people from Britain and Ireland, and how their descendants thrive on challenges, being able to do most things, especially if equipment or supplies are limited. This is how their present, world-famous agricultural economy was built up; and it is such qualities as those of the colonizers and their descendants that are most esteemed by New Zealanders today. Their perfection is found in such mythic heroes as Sir Edmund Hillary, the first person to climb Mount Everest, and Peter Blake of world yachting fame.

Myths however can encourage people to be very selective about what they remember from history, leading them to block out of their minds historical events or experiences which do not fit their cherished stories. The following two examples illustrate this:

Examples

1. In the creation mythology of the United States, the Great Seal of the nation reminds Americans that God or some extraordinary Destiny called them to participate in a new Exodus, a journey from poverty and oppression in other nations to sharing in the building of a society in a new Promised Land based on justice, democracy, and plenty for all. The idea that Americans have been called by God to participate in this work of building, while others struggle in abject poverty and oppression elsewhere, instills in them a sense of pride or nationalism.

However, this myth is very selective: it conceals massive cultural and racial bullying. In the founding of the nation, freedom and justice did *not* extend to the indigenous peoples. They were ruthlessly dispossessed of their lands, even massacred on occasion. African peoples were enslaved and other minorities subsequently have also suffered from widespread prejudice and discrimination. The myth of freedom hence applies to only some of the people; other people who are not regarded as belonging are violently rejected, bullied, or oppressed.[3]

2. White Australians of Anglo-Saxon or Celtic origin have their own founding story articulated in Banjo Paterson's popular lyric *Waltzing Matilda*. It influences their behavior even to this day. In the story, there are two main characters — the squatter, who represents powerful interests in the nation, and the swagman, who symbolizes the underdog in Australian society. The swagman is caught stealing a sheep so the squatter calls up the troopers to catch him, but the thief, refusing to be caught, commits suicide.

At first sight, the squatter appears to have won. Not so! The ghost of society's underdog — or "battler" — continues to haunt Australian legislators and others, reminding them of the needs of the underprivileged in the nation. The qualities of the swagman (an anti-authoritarian, mischievous person) are in every Australian hero: egalitarian individualism, the desire for a "fair-go" for all, ingenuity, modesty, defiance, common sense, and the ability to deflate all forms of pomposity.[4] Fine! but the myth is applied selectively and contains the seeds of violence or intimidation towards "outsiders," such as Aboriginal peoples and asylum seekers.

One of the primary functions of a culture is to provide people with a sense of meaning, *order* and predictability — qualities of life which most people value and, consequently, fear losing. But two things operate in the unconscious of a group and its members: a tendency to mold people according to an order based on the group's symbols and myths, and a tendency to punish or bully those who are different or refuse to submit to this order. A culture's myths, as we have seen, can turn the culture into an object of a people's nationalist worship; anyone who disagrees is apt to be violently — emotionally, intellectually, or physically — rejected.

Three models of cultures which promote bullying

Scientists use models to describe complex phenomena in relatively simple terms. Such models do not perfectly represent reality but they do highlight its most distinctive aspects. Anthropologists accordingly use models to highlight the elements emphasized in cultures but omit nuanced explanations or details. A particular custom, for example, scapegoating, may be defined as belonging to one cultural model yet be omitted from the description of others, not simply because it does not occur in all cultures but because it is less prominent in some of them. Hence, models describe basic patterns but not necessarily fine detail. Let us now look at three models of culture, namely, the hierarchical, the win/lose and the change/malaise models.

1. The hierarchical culture model

In this model, the boundaries of the group and the style of interpersonal relationships within it are sharply defined. People are expected to fit into a tradition-based system in which superiors are presumed to have a monopoly over knowledge by right; subordinates are expected to conform and be dependent. For example, detailed and rigid, morally sanctioned rules about how the human body (and thus the social body) is to be controlled are exemplified in codes regarding dress and posture. Any infraction of such rules is seen as a dangerous expression of individuality. In brief, people fear to break customs lest the group punish them by, for example, ostracizing or ridiculing them.

The leaders' task is fundamentally disciplinary, that is, to maintain adherence to traditional rules and regulations. To carry out such a task, personal charismatic qualities are not needed — in fact, they may be deleterious to the maintenance of the culture because such qualities may draw subordinates away from tradition to a cult of the leader and set precedents which could undermine the status quo. In hierarchical cultures, there is no consultation in decision-making; instead, commands are handed down and are expected to be obeyed without question. Women typically occupy inferior positions in this model because the esteemed qualities of leaders are assumed to be masculine, namely, rationality and aggressive ability to command and enforce conformity.

Examples of this model of culture are governmental bureaucracies, police forces, and armies. The latter two strongly emphasize the maintenance of a chain of command, disciplinary rules, formal training that gives priority to conformity to tradition, and hierarchical authority structures.

There is considerable potential for hierarchical cultures to facilitate bullying, especially when the "power distance" (the degree to which subordinates accept its uneven distribution of power) is marked. In such cases, a small number of superiors is able to control the avenues of communication and hence to cover up any abusive action. Members who have complaints become cynical about ever being listened to impartially and, consequently, feel oppressed. They can feel demeaned, of little importance in the system, and unable to do anything to rectify problems. The bully who is a superior can act with little or no organizational restraints or accountability.[5]

From national governments to university academic departments, large corporations to local employee unions, where authority structures are hierarchical, individual power-holders have the potential to use their officially sanctioned, legitimate power *over* others in illegitimate ways, especially for personal gain.[6] Over recent years in Australia, for example, there have been significant instances of the illegitimate use of power in the armed forces, police, and financial corporations. Thus in 2001, the Australian defence force warned its 50,000 personnel that bullying would not be tolerated; within various Australian police forces, Royal Commissions have uncovered corruption and bullying;[7] and in huge financial corporations, boards, and shareholders have been bullied by directors and others because they were denied the essential information they needed to make decisions.

Other research findings about the bullying elements of this culture highlight the following:

• *The reinforcement of male domination*. Hierarchical organizations are modeled on traditional patriarchal family systems in which males dominate.[8] Some researchers conclude, therefore, that cultures resembling this model legitimize violence by men against women, and that male domination in society is maintained by such forms of violence against women as domestic abuse, rape, and pornography.[9]

• *The concealment of misdemeanors*. Because a primary task of leaders is the maintenance of tradition, there is a built-in potential in this culture for leaders to conceal their own misdemeanors, and those of their colleagues, from public scrutiny. Exposure of such abuse would risk public ridicule of the entire organizational culture. The use of internal and public accountability systems consequently may be vigorously discouraged.

When the model of hierarchical decision-making does not allow or foster consultation, those lower down on the chain of command may become cynical about reporting corruption. They fear they will not be listened to or branded as troublemakers and betrayers of the group. Studies of police corruption in the United States and Australia aptly illustrate this point.[10]

• *The discouragement of creativity*. Allied to the leader's desire to maintain the status quo is a desire not to initiate change. Consequently, anyone in the organization who dares to be creative may be excluded.

• *Unquestioning obedience*. Customs may be so rigid and detailed that people feel suffocated or coerced by tradition and discouraged from making decisions for themselves, or they can refuse to take responsibility for their actions simply by saying that they were "only carrying out orders."

This was the case with Adolf Eichmann who supervised concentration camps under Hitler. "When I received an order," he said, "I obeyed. An oath is an oath. In the observance of that oath I was uncompromising."[11]

• *Impersonal bureaucracies*. Bureaucracy emphasizes seniority and the close observance of impersonal, detailed regulations. The dangers are real: clients can feel they are only inanimate objects or mere statistics; their particular needs can be ignored because the staff who serve them have the attitude that "the rules must be maintained and adhered to," therefore no variations in service are offered to meet their needs.

• *Authoritarian recruits*. Authoritarian or bullying persons are attracted to organizations with cultures of this type and their recruitment reinforces such organizations' coercive qualities.

 Examples

1. "Non-productive people" and neglect

Cultures resembling this model emphasize the qualities of youth and productivity excessively. Consequently, people such as the elderly, the retired, those with physical or intellectual disabilities, prisoners, children of poor families, or others who are not young or productive are in danger of being marginalized. Because such people are considered productively unimportant, it is easy for them to be overlooked by government aid services. Since society is less interested in them, they are more likely to be abused and have little or no opportunity to obtain collective political support for their plight. Aging, for example, is presented as a social problem, and elderly people are talked about as though they were unable to decide matters for themselves and have to have things done for them, rather than with and by them.[12] Similarly, this is the case for people with intellectual or physical disabilities. This is discriminatory, excluding people from enjoying their rights to self-respect and responsible decision-making as far as their health permits.

People who are dying also create a "problem" and a subtle form of bullying occurs against them. Hospitals according to this culture model are to keep people alive; death is, in a sense, a mark of failure, especially since death is seen to be an unsolved problem of medical engineering. A dying patient becomes increasingly a *passive* agent in his or her own death, a "puppet" in a "play" in which the principal actors are the medical staff and the relatives of the dying person. Doctors and family members hesitate to tell the person that death is imminent. They fear hurting the sensibilities, or lowering the morale, of the suffering person who daily becomes more and more like a lonely child, rather than an adult involved in the most important process of his or her life. The dying person's family and friends become increasingly isolated or alienated from the patient. They are apt to feel, as they surround the dying person's bed, that they are trespassing on foreign territory: they are attending a person who is dying in an institution that is primarily concerned with healing the sick and returning them to regular society. Dying and death are seen as signs of institutional failure.[13] Sociologist David Dempsey claims: "The essence of the family's game is pretense ... Appearances are kept up; there is much small talk and forced cheerfulness while the basic feelings, the things that cry out in the heart, go unsaid."[14]

2. The Catholic Church before the Second Vatican Council

All organizations (including the churches) in which hierarchy is entrenched, resemble this model. Prior to the Second Vatican Council (1962–1965) the Catholic Church emphasized many of the qualities of this culture model.[15] Church membership was hierarchically graded: pope, bishops, priests, religious, and laity. The laity were to be passive recipients of the expert religious leadership of the clergy and to go about saving their souls in a dangerous, secular world through their faithful observance of a set of intricate rules and customs. Sin was often regarded as synonymous with the breaking of formal regulations, for example, eating meat on Fridays or attending a non-Catholic liturgy without ecclesiastical permission. God was presented as the stern, remote Almighty, and Unchanging One, Creator/Regulator — the God of the Old Testament, instilling fear in people; and Jesus Christ as the King, Savior and Judge of a people who break "the rules"; while Mary, the Mother of God, and all the other saints were depicted in contrasting fashion as approachable and understanding beings.

By depicting God the Father as more like a divine bully whose primary aim was to instil fear in people, and in exaggerating Jesus' role as judge and downplaying his compassionate, merciful presence, such a church culture was obviously open to abuse. There was the constant danger that external conformity to rules was more important than a personal relationship with the Lord, and that morality was more concerned with avoiding private sins than with tackling social issues of justice and human rights. Clergy could avoid accountability for their actions by claiming they had a role sanctified by God and tradition and so were not answerable to laity and the Church as a whole. Theologian (now Cardinal) Avery Dulles commented: "[We] may acknowledge ... those who hold office will commonly be tempted to employ their power in a dominative and manipulative way. They can easily tend to sacrifice other values to the demands of law and order and to misconceive of loyalty as if it meant merely passive conformity."[16]

To conclude, Joan Chittister, a Benedictine Sister, writing on institutional prejudice against women, commented that "nowhere are women actually equal, either in the Church or society, and every-where male systems define, restrict and exclude women from their inner sanctums in which decisions are made, even about women."[17]

2. The win/lose culture model

In this type of culture people are individualistic, utilitarian, and competitive yet egalitarian, but they have a very weak sense of belonging or of having obligations to the group or institution. People obtain their personal identity from submitting to, and interiorizing, the clearly stated norms and goals of their society's inner structure. Individuals form alliances with one another to provide better opportunities for success, but such alliances are very fragile, since they are held together only for the self-interest of the individuals themselves. These alliances break apart once more strategically profitable relationships develop.

Individualism and unrestrained, aggressive competi-tiveness set the scene for a culture in which people and institutions are encouraged to bully one another for their own personal advantage. The gender emphasis is masculine because the qualities thought to be required for success are aggressiveness, rationality, and individualism. Bullying can be an esteemed sign of courage and manliness. The ultimate goal is success symbolized by the material goods one can amass. "Sin" lies in negligence or in the individual's own mistakes in pursuing their mission to succeed or to achieve their destiny; it is the failure to take advantage of this or that relationship which will guarantee economic, social, or political advantage over others. Morality is reduced to what can be called the "Watergate mentality," that is, "do everything to get ahead, without concern for the common good, provided you are not found out." The Canadian social commentator John Ralston Saul argues that the win/lose culture model flourishes in contemporary political and business circles. Leaders are almost without exception bullies and have great difficulty coming to terms with the democratic process, setting enormous value upon secrecy in their abuse of power.[18]

Jealousy and envy operate powerfully in this culture model, motivating people to become bullies. Because such emotions are selfish and malevolent, they have destructive results. Bullies will destroy what they cannot get or hold on to, for example, in the closing months of World War II, Hitler ordered the destruction of cities he occupied before surrendering them. Indonesian forces similarly went on destructive rampages prior to their expulsion from East Timor.

Cultures of this model encourage institutional violence towards the poor and weak in society, people whom governments regard as irrelevant or harmful to the achievement of success by the powerful. The assumption is that people are poor through their own fault and should be punished accordingly, by depriving them of all welfare assistance.

Examples: corporate cultures of abuse

Organizations based on enterprise capitalism resemble this win/lose model. Their pivotal myth is faith in the unhindered operation of market competition, born out of the false belief that the market is a self-regulating mechanism. The impact on employees (and their families) can be devastating, as can be seen in the two broad subcultures of sacrifice and of blame.

1. In the *subculture of sacrifice*,[19] employees are expected to give their all to their companies, even if it means sacrificing their family life. Burnout, absenteeism and other signs of stress are common. These are seen as signs of weakness in employees who are treated as disposable "objects" when they cannot cope any longer. In some companies employees are expected to accept abuse from their superiors. Business consultants Lesley Wright and Marti Smye comment: "It is similar to the hazing that passes for initiation rites in … secret societies. Unless you have been humiliated in public, you are not considered part of the team. Employees … look forward to the day when they can do it themselves."[20]

2. The other broad subculture of abuse within the win/lose model is the *subculture of blame*. When there is little or no team work in an organization, individual employees may be rewarded or blamed for what happens within it, though the employers may absolve themselves from faulty leadership. Employees may in some cases have no right of appeal, and may be summarily dismissed. This creates a constant bullying climate of uncertainty and fear.

In the United States, free-market principles have fostered such subcultures of sacrifice or blame where public ownership is kept to a minimum and welfare services for the poor provide only a limited safety net. Trade unions are commonly kept weak, indicating a fear that vigorous labor organizations interfere with market mechanisms and the maximization of profits.

3. The change/malaise culture model

Significant cultural change involves a cycle of three inter-related stages: an *initial* stage, a *malaise-evoking* stage, and a *move forward* stage. Progress through these stages within any one cycle is generally extremely slow and filled with fears, uncertainties, and dangers. In the second stage in particular there is considerable potential for violence or the abuse of power. At some point, people must choose either to escape backwards to the assumed securities of the past, becoming paralyzed by the malaise, or they must take the risk to move forward into an uncertain future. People who persevere with a cycle of change and have arrived at the third stage look back and recognize that the chaos of the previous stage had been a painful blessing. They used the breakdown of the old certitudes in the second stage as a chance to rethink and create radically new ways of living and working together. Much of our explanation of the culture/malaise model will focus on this second stage, that is, the *malaise-evoking* or *malaise* stage.

In the malaise stage, people have a sense of belonging to their group but there is a marked lack of agreement about the ways in which they are to relate to one another because in the course of breaking down its culture, its roles have become thoroughly confused. Internal cohesion is weak and social conflict is considerable. Political and social cliques, alliances, mafia-type organizations, and gangs form in response to people's needs for security and control.

People are suspicious of one another, feeling that others are manipulating the system against them. It is a climate in which bullying against others who dare to be different flourishes. This type of behavior characterizes the countries of the former Soviet Union: once order imposed from the top disintegrates there are no internally acceptable structures to replace it.

The novel *Lord of the Flies* by William Golding, also describes the dynamics of the malaise stage. On the island in the story, a group of boys, freed from the normal regimentation of a traditional English school culture, engages in the most vicious forms of bullying, with individuals colluding to avoid being victims themselves. Golding shows how bullying is an evil tendency dormant in human nature: although the world may appear a bright place, the corruption of violence can suddenly erupt from within people and darken it.

THE RECENT CULTURAL REVOLUTION AND THE RISE OF THE NEW RIGHT

The Western world experienced something like a widespread cultural malaise in the 1960s and 1970s when, as a consequence of a cultural revolution, values and institutions held sacred for five centuries were questioned. It was a turbulent time. Nothing was considered too precious to be questioned, the churches included. In response to this cultural malaise, now further exacerbated by the disorienting influences of ongoing globalization, many people in politics and commerce chose to go back to the past and to revitalize nineteenth-century capitalism. Terminology may have changed, but not the reality of fundamental capitalism in which the free market determines economic activity and governments serve primarily to remove obstacles to its smooth functioning. This major reactionary movement in the Western world is variously referred to by such titles as the New Right, economic rationalism,[21] market capitalism, neoclassical-capitalism, and market liberalism. It is an ideological political reaction to the perceived vagueness and moral malaise at the end of the modern era: it has a distinctive set of values and imposes clear-cut answers to contemporary social and economic challenges. Everything must again be measured in terms of "the bottom line"; profit is the sole measure of value and the economics profession serves as its priesthood.

In brief, the New Right is a revitalization in contemporary clothes of virtually unrestrained capitalism.[22] Public institutions are changed into pseudo-businesses trading in, for example, healthcare and education. The dramatic rise of for-profit hospitals in the United States in recent years is an example of this economic ideology: financial return to shareholders, not the quality of service to patients, is their primary aim. This philosophy is now popular even in Britain, Canada, Australia, and New Zealand, countries which had previously modified the worst features of capitalism through their respective developments of the welfare state.[23]

The term *welfare state* describes a state with a combination of direct or indirect benefits and services whose purpose is to improve the well-being of citizens. A welfare state assumes that all citizens have rights to healthcare and employment, and that it is the task of governments to provide structures to enable these rights to be enjoyed: governments committed to a welfare state aim to relieve poverty and reduce inequality by assuring a minimum level of financial aid through social security and unemployment benefits.

Economic rationalism, which repudiates the welfare state philosophy, has been succinctly defined as "a government's free-market approach to economic management typically reflected in the adoption of privatization, deregulation, user pays, and low government spending as indicators of economic success."[24] There is no room in a free-market economy for the values of the welfare state.

The social consequences of economic rationalism and the shift away from the welfare state are invariably the same: poor people become poorer and more marginalized by society. This is a form of *structural* bullying.

• In *Britain* it is claimed that the government's policies over recent years have given priority to the "productive," who "produce goods and services that can be profitably marketed," and the marginalized or "parasitic," who "are either dependent on state benefits or whose economic activities are deemed 'unprofitable' in narrowly conceived terms."[25] It is claimed that in the 1980s and 1990s the "health gaps between the rich and poor, between social classes, between north and south, and between the inner city and shire counties have all widened."[26]

• In *Australia*, a similar pattern is beginning to emerge. Australian health policy-makers have gradually shifted their concern from equity and social justice to cost containment and, more recently, to cost-effectiveness.[27] Primary care such as health promotion and education is being de-emphasized and particular groups, for example, the aged, Aboriginal peoples, and individuals who are mentally sick or have physical disabilities are being increasingly marginalized. They lack the political and economic power to be heard when they cry out about their plight. Economic rationalism, with its emphasis on the importance of efficiency, is becoming an increasingly influential force that might ultimately destroy the present Australia-wide insurance system.[28] Peter Saunders, Professor of Social Policy at the University of New South Wales, comments: "The logic of market competition leaves little room for the state to play anything other than a marginal role, supporting those unable to fend for themselves in a competitive market environment with a series of residual, under-funded and stigmatizing programs."[29] Indeed a new underclass of people in absolute poverty is emerging in many Western countries where, for decades, such poverty has not existed. Saunders finds that, despite positive economic indications, economic liberalism in Australia has contributed to increases in unemployment, inequality, social dysfunction, and alienation.

Economic rationalists would simply like to forget or hide people who are poor because they distract successful profit-seekers from their task of acquiring more and more. Hence, denial is a way they use to cope with the challenges they present. The Australian Prime Minister, John Howard (1996–), for example, would deny the genocidal racism directed in the past against Aboriginal peoples: "I sympathize fundamentally with Australians who are insulted when they are told that we have a racist, bigoted past. And Australians are told that quite regularly. Our children are taught that."[30] Many would agree with him.[31]

• In *healthcare in general*, the biomedical model that economic rationalists favor is also ill-equipped to relate to the health problems of people who are poor: the body is likened to a machine that is to be healed through medical, technological, and scientific processes. The *social* model of healthcare, by contrast, assumes that the patterns of health and disease are largely the product of economic and cultural influences such as racism and social discrimination. It is such issues as these that must be addressed, otherwise it will be impossible to provide long-term healing services to poor people. But not only is the biomedical model unable to address these issues: it is also unable to touch the inner pain of low self-worth and hopelessness that structural poverty or bullying produces in people who are poor.[32]

• Government policies concerning *refugees, asylum seekers,* and *law breakers* are also increasingly being driven by the anti-poor attitude of the New Right. Refugees and asylum seekers are thought to threaten national identity and economic prosperity and are treated accordingly. Law breakers are rapidly incarcerated in the attempt to move problem cases quickly out of sight.

The introduction of mandatory sentencing and zero tolerance policies, the re-establishment of children's prisons and the movement of young offenders to adult courts are all aimed at restricting the discretionary judgments of judges and social workers. Sectors of the population singled out as most in need of control and retribution are the welfare poor, minority peoples, unemployed persons, and marginalized working-class youth.[33] Commenting on the Australian scene, legal experts David Brown and Meredith Wilkie conclude that "as a broad generalization, from the mid-1980s through the 1990s, a new retributivism was played out in penal and sentencing policies ... Among the effects ... has been the muting of the voices of prisoners and a lack of political interest in prisoners and prison conditions other than as manifestations of a convenient 'other' against which to vent a range of anxieties and insecurities and a site of tabloid fantasies of 'motel conditions' and taxpayer funded 'luxury.' "[34]

SCAPEGOATING

Devaluing and scapegoating the powerless is another abusive mechanism people often use in times of change. Scapegoating or witch-hunting is the process of naming, searching for, and eliminating agents believed to be causing harm. Although those named as being the causes of harm may not have actually been causing any harm, naming is still done because it gives those who blame others a sense of control: causes of problems are "found," problems become somehow more comprehensible and the fuzzy anxiety generated by unspecified threats is curbed.[35]

Scapegoating exists at all times and in all cultures, but is especially prominent in change cycles during their malaise stage. In fact, the greater the social upheaval and consequent fear of the unknown, the more frequent and persistent the witch-hunting or scapegoating.

 Examples

As the use of money became more widespread in Europe in the Middle Ages, the involuntary poor became starkly, socially defined because of their lack of it. The presence of the poor though caused the rich to fear that they would lose their own wealth through vengeance. Therefore, the poor were identified and marginalized, lest they endanger the emerging wealthy class simply by their presence. Hence, in the late Middle Ages, when considerable animosity towards the poor developed, oppressive legislation was introduced against them.[36]

Later again, in the Great Depression of the 1930s, the Jews in Germany provided a convenient scapegoat that Hitler could use as the reason for Germany's economic woes.

Accusers avoid guilt

When people name a scapegoat for their anxiety and misfortunes, they relieve themselves of any guilt for what unpleasant changes may be happening around them. They lay the blame simplistically on others, believing that if others can be named as culprits and then punished, their tribulations will disappear. The scapegoat is branded as evil and inferior and not worth being treated as fully human, so their punishment is seen to serve the common good. The scapegoat is presumed to be manipulating others to obtain control of resources or to get revenge for being marginalized; and their accusers are prejudged to be in the right. In transferring guilt to others, bullies and their supporters project onto the victims their own internal evil which they cannot face themselves (e.g., envy, selfishness, greed, or manipulation of power). The true villains lie within human persons, but few people want to look there because doing so would demand painful internal conversion and changes in how they live. Many also do not do the hard work of analyzing the complex changes occurring in the wider society that are causing their fears, such as the rise of globalization.

Scapegoats on the margins of society

Witches or scapegoats — those believed to be causing the loss of security — have usually been the same type of people throughout history: people on the margins of society, such as academics, prophets or other known nonconformists, creative people who challenge traditional ways of thinking or doing things, and those who have no access to power structures. Scapegoating occurs in *all* human organizations. I myself have found it among academics who publicly pride themselves on their rationality and commitment to truth and in voluntary organizations committed to the teachings of Jesus Christ! Commonly, the person who is treated as a scapegoat is someone who may be annoying people and is already on the margins, lacking power for self-defense.

In politics, those on the margins are ready-made targets, for example, migrants, refugees, people who are poor, and women. Throughout Western society, political parties are proposing simplistic solutions to complex problems arising from globalization and postmodernity, and they are blaming indigenous peoples, migrants, refugees, and the poor for their economic and social fears and insecurities. Throughout Europe over the last decade, right wing political parties with anti-immigration messages have grown rapidly and anti-immigrant crime has jumped alarmingly. In Australia in the late 1990s, the politician Pauline Hanson tapped into the same fears in the formation of her "One Nation" Party. She argued for zero net immigration, an end to multiculturalism, restoration of the so called Anglo-Celtic cultural tradition, the abolition of native title to land, and the cessation of special Aboriginal funding programs.[37]

Populist power of the leader

In witch-hunting crazes such as those now sweeping the world, the leader or chief bully has tremendous power, but they will survive only as long as they have the support of enough people with a desire for simplistic solutions and a fear of losing control. Hitler could not have persecuted the Jews, or Senator McCarthy innocent people in the early 1950s in the United States, without a power base from which to begin. A bully's gift is the ability to feel the malaise of people and simplistically to pinpoint a presumed cause. Adopting some of Hanson's racist policies in the federal elections of 2001, the two major parties vied with each other in fueling the nationalist desires of Australians. Information regarding asylum seekers was manipulated or denied for political advantage.[38] However, people are fickle: when a witch-hunt craze dies down, the bully tends to be blamed and they conveniently forget how they conspired with the bully earlier. For example, following the end of World War II, many French people failed to acknowledge how they had colluded with their Nazi occupiers: they suffered a generally accepted collective amnesia about it.

Moral panic and scapegoating

The term "moral panic" is a contemporary expression for scapegoating crazes; it is meant to convey the sense of inappropriateness or unreasonableness of such social reactions. Moral panics erupt in response to significant widespread anxiety and fear and are stimulated often by surprisingly trivial incidents; they are also often encouraged by the mass media.[39] Sociologist Stanley Cohen coined the term and has used it to illustrate the way groups of young people have been stigmatized by the mass media: youths who imitated the styles of dress of others who had committed isolated but highly publicized misdemeanors were excluded from job opportunities and places of entertainment, or even taken into custody by the police. For example, in the 1950s, those affecting Edwardian dress were dubbed "teddy boys"; in the 1960s, those dressing as sophisticates were dubbed "Mods" and those sporting leather jackets, "rockers."[40] By stigmatizing people who wore particular styles of clothing, people in general can contentedly distract themselves from negative developments in the economy of society at large.

More recent examples of moral panics are the reactions to immigrants and refugees. The power that the media exercise in moral panics can adversely affect innocent people whose actions are condemned without trial.

Example: the contemporary Catholic Church as a culture of change/malaise

Contemporary critics of the Catholic Church may feel as Cardinal John Henry Newman did in 1843: "You must bear in mind that, if I speak strongly in various places ... against the existing state of things [in the Church], it is not wantonly, but to show I feel the difficulties which certain minds are distressed with."[41] Many Catholics feel saddened or anguished at what they see happening in their Church today. They feel that there is a pastoral inertia, apathy, and a loss of opportunities to evangelize the postmodern world. They see friends and family members walk away from it as it fails, they feel, to speak compassionately to them and their needs. They hear of sex scandals that have been covered up for years. People are being bullied, scapegoated' and stigmatized as "dangerous feminists" or "unorthodox theologians" simply because they raise critically important questions about how to evangelize contemporary secular societies. For many, the Church is going backwards and retreating to the fortress world of the time before the Second Vatican Council. Readily do they identify with the cry of the prophet Jeremiah as he contemplated the destruction of all that was dear to him and to Israel: "My anguish, my anguish! I writhe in pain! Oh, the walls of my heart! My heart is beating wildly; I cannot keep silent ... Distaster overtakes disaster, the whole land is laid waste" (Jeremiah 4:19-20).

What reasons can we give for the turmoil in the Catholic Church? As a cultural anthropologist, I find the pain of concerned Catholics and the existence of the contemporary turmoil quite understandable, even inevitable. The Second Vatican Council set in motion not just a theological revolution, but a cultural one. The culture model that best describes what is happening in the Catholic Church is the *change/malaise* model, and the Catholic Church is in the malaise-evoking stage, with its members experiencing all the tensions typical of that stage. Though there are hesitant signs of the third or *move forward* stage beginning to emerge, the Catholic Church is almost overwhelmed by tensions and divisions. Why?

Two principles would seem to help explain this. Firstly, culture is primarily about providing people with stability, a sense of felt order; any change in the interpretation of its founding story, no matter how urgently it may be needed, will inevitably evoke cultural chaos accompanied by the breakdown of identity, scapegoating, and movement backwards to a "golden past." Secondly, the Second Vatican Council restored the Church's founding story. This led to cultural turmoil; the interiorization of such narratives and their concrete cultural expression is a very long and tortuous process.

The Second Vatican Council was an effort to reform the Catholic Church at its most basic level of identity; the Council sought to bring it back to its authentic founding story. For the very best theological reasons, it exposed the inadequacies of the interpretation of its founding story which had been lived for at least the previous three hundred years. Hence, the model of the Catholic Church as hierarchical had to be balanced by the requirements of the Church as the People of God. Likewise, the priesthood as a sacrament and ministry had to be balanced with the fact that, by baptism, all are priests. The Council did not, and could not, describe precisely how the equilibrium between the many polarities in its documents was to be achieved. For generations, many of the faithful had been childishly conforming to the detailed instructions of clerical elders and then, overnight, they were given a mandate — laity included — to act on their own initiative as creative evangelizers, finding and maintaining the balance between the polarities in the documents of the

Council, such as those relating to the hierarchical structure of the Church, on the one hand, and its members as the People of God, on the other. Little wonder that the turmoil occurred — and it continues!

To complicate matters further, the Council ended as the postmodern cultural revolution was assaulting the Western world. The Catholic Church, which had been hidden from modernity, let alone postmodernity, was thoroughly ill-equipped to adjust positively to changes in broader society.

The theologian Yves Congar said, after the Second Vatican Council, that it would take at least fifty years for a Council such as this one to begin to bear fruit.[42] To an anthropologist this makes sense but, sadly, organizations, including the Catholic Church, do not move automatically from the second to the third stage of cultural change, the "move forward" stage. In the present chaos of the Catholic Church, the dominant reaction is what I call *restorationism*, that is, an uncritical reaffirmation of structures and attitudes which existed prior to the Second Vatican Council in response to the malaise and stress resulting from the theological and cultural turmoil generated by the Council and the postmodern world at large.

Restorationism takes many forms, some fanatically aggressive and others less so. All forms are marked by intolerance to opposition; dialogue is rarely possible with its advocates. There are, in other words, many signs of a culture of bullying. In this case, there are attempts to re-establish a monocultural Rome-centered Church rather than to encourage the development of a multicultural one giving greater say to the College of Bishops; and there are appointments of bishops without appropriate consultation, an emphasis on theological orthodoxy at the expense of pastoral creativity, and the encouragement of fundamentalist groups.

Those adhering to this model of Church overlook the Council's outward-looking thrust to the world and the subsequent, quite radical social documents of recent popes. As in all sects, restorationists are elitist and claim alone to have the full truth. Their intolerance of other Catholics who disagree with them fosters a witch-hunt mentality against those who dare to question their views. Victims of such bullying behavior have included various liberation and feminist theologians and social justice advocates.[43]

Summary

1. The causes of bullying are deep not just within the history of individual bullies but also in human cultures. Cultures restrain people from acting in certain ways broadly regarded as unacceptable yet they can also legitimize them to act violently.

2. The shared meanings, values, symbols, and myths of a culture establish strong ties among its members which distinguish those who are culturally "in" from those branded as "outsiders." This tends to legitimize people to act in bullying ways towards those named as "outsiders."

3. The hierarchical, win/lose and change/malaise models of culture are three ways different cultures of bullying may be described.

4. Globalization is evoking widespread identity and security crises among the peoples of the world. People lacking the power to have their needs made known, including the poor and minorities, are being stigmatized and marginalized by a revitalization of nineteenth century capitalism.

5. The Catholic Church is in a state of cultural breakdown as it searches to implement guiding principles enunciated by the Second Vatican Council. Although the Church is a divine institution as well as a human one, it suffers from the *human* abuse of power.

Questions

1. Can you identify a time when you felt the power of culture in your own life? It could have been in your observation of differences in lifestyle between your family and relatives compared to the broader society around you or it could have been when you were visiting another country and could not speak the language or found the food not according to your taste. What did the experience of a different culture feel like?

2. What is the culture of the organization you work for? Does it resemble one of the models described in this chapter?

3. In your organization or your country, are any individuals or groups being scapegoated? If so, why do you think they are chosen as scapegoats?

4. Read Mark 14:32-42 (Jesus in agony in the Garden of Gethsemane). Does fear play any part in the Church's attempt to live out its mission of proclaiming the Good News of God's reign?

Chapter 4

A Gospel Response

If only there were evil people somewhere
insidiously committing evil deeds,
and it were necessary only to separate them
from the rest of us
and destroy them.
But the line dividing good and evil
cuts through the heart of every human being...
Alexander Solzenitsyn[1]

When he saw the crowds, he had compassion for them,
because they were harassed and helpless.
Matthew 9:36

This chapter explains:

☛ Jesus ministered to people caught up in a culture of bullying

☛ five principles for preventing bullying from arising

☛ five practical ways victims may respond constructively to bullying

☛ five practical ways non-victims may assist victims.

Jesus' teaching and life in general opposed and undermined bullying, but to appreciate just how radical his teaching was, it is helpful to remember certain aspects of the society in which he lived. Palestine in the first Christian century was in political and religious turmoil. It showed many of the dysfunctional symptoms described in the change/malaise culture model. While Palestine was subject to the Roman Emperor Caesar Augustus, this was only a nominal rule because much of the land was controlled by local elites. Large land holdings were in the hands of Judaean elders, scribes, and high-priestly families. There was no such thing as a middle class. In vivid contrast to the wealthy few, peasants were extremely poor, owning little if no land at all. They were "subjected to bullying, blackmail, and over-taxation" (Luke 3:13-4). "Failure to repay debt could lead to imprisonment" (Matthew 5:25-6).[2]

Given Jesus' radical message of justice for the poor and identification with the victims of violence, it was inevitable that he and his followers would be bullied by the wealthy political elite. Their persistent intimidation began with Herod, the ruthless governor of Galilee who wanted to destroy the newborn Messiah and who was prepared to kill the innocent to do so (Matt 2:1-8). Herod was enraged when the wise men exposed his manipulative scheming. Jesus also experienced mob bullying immediately after he commenced his public ministry. At first, the crowds were deeply impressed by his eloquence but when he said that his healing ministry would extend to non-Jews, many wanted to kill him by throwing him over a cliff (Luke 4:22-30). The Pharisees, members of a sect within Judaism, also frequently harassed Jesus. Unlike Jesus, they believed holiness depended on a meticulous external conformity to detailed rituals and they neglected what Jesus considered fundamental, namely, an interior conversion to God. The Pharisees tried to shame him in public (John 8:3-11), they scapegoated him by calling him Beelzebub, a hated demon (Matthew 12:24), and, finally, they plotted with others (namely the sect of the Saduccees; the Herodians, who were supporters of the Roman invaders; and the people in general, who wanted him to be like other kings) to kill him as a scapegoat for the whole nation (John 18:14).

Five principles for preventing bullying

Let us now explore, by means of a series of five principles, what can be done to prevent bullying. Where appropriate, we will draw on the Scriptures and the social teaching of the Catholic Church.

Principle 1. Recognize that bullying is an evil and an assault on the dignity of the human person.

Evil has been defined as any action that "deprives innocent people of their humanity, from small scale assaults on a person's dignity to outright murder."[3] Hence, any action that deliberately or otherwise seeks to destroy people's self-worth or creates conditions that spiritually, psychologically, or materially diminish their dignity, their sense of self-worth, and their ability to be responsible for their own actions is evil. In short, whatever diminishes people's basic human rights — their rights to food, shelter, security, good name, privacy, freedom — is an evil.[4]

Bullying is an evil because it seeks to take away human dignity, a dignity that comes primarily from the fact that every human being is created in God's image (Genesis 1:27). The human person should not be a commodity, able to be manipulated through historical, economic, or social agencies, and disposed of at will. Rather, each person is called to be an agent of God's loving and creative justice in the world. The psalmist beautifully expresses these two aspects of our dignity and obligation to be wise stewards:

> When I look at your heavens, the work of your fingers…
> what are human beings that you are mindful of them,
> mortals that you care for them?
> Yet you have made them a little lower than God…
> You have given them dominion over the works of your hands;
> you have put all things under their feet (Psalm 8:3-6).

Through the life, death and resurrection of Jesus, this dignity is raised to unimaginable heights: "for in Christ Jesus you are all children of God through faith. As many of you as were baptized into Christ have clothed yourselves with Christ" (Galatians 3:26-27). All people are bonded together through the life of Christ, so that "If one member suffers, all suffer together with it; if one member is honored, all rejoice together with it" (1 Corinthians 12:26). In serving one another, we are serving Christ at the same time; in violating the rights of anyone, we are insulting Christ (Matthew 10:40; 18:5).

Sinful Structures

In Catholic social teaching, cultures of bullying are sometimes referred to as *sinful structures*. A sinful structure is a social habit, institutionalized way of life, or political or economic arrangement or structure which, of its nature, causes injustice to people or leads them knowingly or unknowingly into sinful ways of acting.[5] Examples are laws that deny the sanctity of life before birth, educational systems that do not take into account the special needs of ethnic groups in society or which encourage racism, patriarchal organizations that marginalize and degrade women, healthcare systems that make profit the overriding concern in decision-making, and government health programs that ignore cultural causes of poverty. Liberation theologians (who emphasize the theme of liberation from poverty and oppression in the Bible and who interpret Church teaching in terms of it) highlight the sinful structures that Jesus confronted even in his day; as Jesus identified and judged these structures or cultures as sinful, so today the same judgment must be made.[6]

Pope John Paul II also speaks of the *culture of death*. By this he means a culture that fosters or permits situations of violence, such as: attacks on the earliest stages of life and life in its final stages; violence against children through poverty, malnutrition, and hunger; criminal drug culture; and hatred which results in murder, war, and genocide. To counter this culture of death there must be, he writes, the building of a new culture of life founded on respect for human dignity and justice.[7]

Principle 2. Acknowledge that everyone is capable of bullying because we are all prone to sin. Consequently, we must be vigilant that the disease does not spread from within ourselves or our organizations.

According to the Book of Genesis, the origin of any human evil action is to be found deep within the human heart: "The Lord saw that the wickedness of humankind was great in the earth, and that every inclination of the thoughts of their hearts was only evil continually" (Gen 6:5). Later in the Old Testament, evil is described as being synonymous with immorality and unfaithfulness to the Covenant which God had made with God's people (see 1 Kings 2:44) — or indeed with any action that dehumanizes God's people. The *whole* of God's people, at one point, were considered culturally evil or abusive because they tried to bully God to do what they wanted — but this led to suffering: "Not one of these — not one of this evil generation — shall see the good land that I swore to give your ancestors" (Deuteronomy 1:35).

Selfishness, narcissism, and the desire for power are at the root of bullying; the most grievous evil is the attempt to control or ignore God. Jesus himself describes the deep inner capacity for evil within human nature and that it is an inner battle to avoid egotism and domination over others: "The spirit indeed is willing, but the flesh is weak" (Mark 14:38).[8]

This inner capacity for evil though is no extraordinary phenomenon. The twentieth century political philosopher

Hannah Arendt drew attention to the most frightening and common quality of violators, namely, their often sheer ordinariness. She calls this the "banality of evil." In her description of Adolf Eichmann's trial in Israel, she pointed to the plainness or ordinariness of his life and his views of the world, while everyone around him claimed he was the quintessence of evil.[9] True, the racist rantings of Hitler's writings were shockingly evil, but Eichmann was an ordinary, apparently sane, and unreflective bureaucrat. Tests found he was not mentally ill, surprisingly. As Arendt says: "The trouble with Eichmann was precisely that so many were like him, and that many were neither perverted, nor sadistic, that they were, and still are, terribly and terrifyingly normal."[10] Eichmann's bullying actions were shockingly evil, but as a person he was thoroughly ordinary and apparently not motivated by evil intentions, although he was committed to achieving his personal fulfillment through a bureaucratic career.[11]

Christopher Browning, a social historian, also argues that the great majority of Nazi brutalities were undertaken not by bizarre maniacs, sadists, and "monsters" but instead by ordinary people who happened to have made bad choices in unfortunate circumstances.[12] Bullies can also be apparently quite ordinary people in much of their lives yet revert to sadistic intimidation of their victims when it suits them: gentle and kind one minute, they can be cruel the next.

The monk and prolific writer Thomas Merton (1915–1968) commented that Eichmann's sanity was disturbing. He wrote: "We rely on the sane people of the world to preserve it from barbarism, madness, destruction. And now it begins to dawn on us that it is precisely the *sane* ones who are the most dangerous ... If modern man [*sic*]... were a little less sane, a little more doubtful ... perhaps there might be a possibility of his survival."[13] A disturbing conclusion to these reflections by Arendt, Browning, and Merton is that each one of us has the potential to commit evil, given the right circumstances. John Bradford said it well in the sixteenth century when he saw some criminals being led to execution: "But for the grace of God, there goes John Bradford."

The way from localized or small-scale evil to large-scale evil in the world is often a sequence of small, ordinary, seemingly harmless steps made by people who commonly remain ignorant of their contributions to such perversity. Again, apparently sane people are involved in widespread compromises that form cultures of oppression. Individually, the compromises may seem small to the perpetrators but, objectively, they lead to a culture that legitimizes people to bully.

Examples of incremental evil

1. Consider the stock market insider trading scandals of the 1980s. People were tempted to make dramatic financial returns by easily breaking the rules of banking and investment in apparently small ways. So many people gave in to the temptation that the entire financial structure of the world was threatened and consequently many innocent people around the world suffered. They felt bullied by a banking system that they had, until then, trusted.[14]

2. The global climate today is significantly and adversely affected by the outpouring of carbon dioxide into the atmosphere through the production and use of industrial gases, inorganic fertilizers, and cars.[15] Most of us drive cars but what are we doing to prevent air pollution from worsening? Why do we collude in fostering environmental calamity? It is not that we set out intentionally to bully the innocent of today and future generations by destroying our environment but, by merely colluding with the maintenance of the status quo, we contribute to collective bullying. Even if we become aware of what is happening, we can give in to laziness and narcissism. We don't want to be bothered. We are content to let someone else change the situation.[16]

Principle 3. Understand that God has a preferential love for the victim and so must the followers of Christ.

In the Scriptures, God identifies preferentially with the victims of violence but not with sinners or the perpetrators of violence. Ironically, however, much of Christian tradition has emphasized the relationship between the perpetrator or *sinner* and God; not much has been said of the *victim* except in relation to their need to forgive their oppressor.[17]

The quintessential biblical victim is the poor person because they do not have access to the political processes that would enable them to agitate for changes to their situation. They are victims of cultures of bullying which contain all the elements we have explored, including marginalization or exclusion from society and deprivation of self-worth. Since the rich and powerful declare the poor to be non-persons, they discriminate against them for their own selfish ends with impunity. But God does not collude with such arrogance. Let us look more closely then at the nature of cultural bullying in the Christian Scriptures and at God's preferential love for the victims of bullying.

The societies described in the Scriptures were polarized: wealth was concentrated in the hands of minorities while the rest of the people lived according to a subsistence economy or in degrading poverty. Those who lived in poverty faced two important realities: the dire lack of material goods necessary for life and the lack of power to defend themselves and their kin from the oppression of the wealthy. The poor were made to feel inferior and unwanted in societies that defined status in terms of wealth. People remained in poverty because of the arrogance and avarice of the rich who were corrupted through storing up treasures for themselves and who were not "rich toward God" (Luke 12:21).

Jewish people were aware of two types of poverty: poverty as a social or structural *disease* and poverty as a personal *illness*. As a structural or social disease, poverty referred to such things as the lack of material goods and social marginalization. Poverty as an illness, by contrast, meant the inner spiritual and psychological pain of, for example, the loss of self-worth due to social marginalization and the accompanying feelings of powerlessness. As an illness, poverty is dramatically evident in the lamentations of the people during the Babylonian exile (in the sixth and fifth centuries before the common era). Ponder the inner pain of lostness in the following excerpt from Psalm 137. The feeling of alienation or depression of the exiles in a foreign land due to the destruction of the three fundamental foundations of their culture, that is, kingship, Jerusalem, and temple, so overwhelmed them that they had no heart to sing their traditional songs:

> By the rivers of Babylon —
> there we sat down and there we wept
> when we remembered Zion.
> On the willows there
> we hung up our harps.
> For there our captors asked us for songs,
> and our tormentors asked for mirth, saying,
> "Sing us one of the songs of Zion!"
> How could we sing the Lord's song
> in a foreign land? (Psalm 137:1-4).

Later in Palestine, when Jesus healed people, he was concerned about both the social *and* personal aspects of poverty. Hence, the blind man went from "sitting by the roadside" (Luke 18:35), a condition symbolic of social marginalization, to being healed by Jesus and subsequently following him *on* the road, a condition symbolic of inner healing (cf. Luke 18:43).[18]

Returning though to the Old Testament, there we read how structural poverty, with its accompanying dehumanization of the people, is contrary to God's covenant with the people: human persons are equal in dignity before God, so all have a right to an equitable use of this world's resources and all are called to work collaboratively to ensure this is respected. The test of a community's faithfulness to God is its concrete daily respect for these truths. "You shall love the Lord God," says the Lord in describing the heart of the covenant relationship with the Israelites, "and keep his charge, his decrees, his ordinances, and his commandments always" (Deut 11:1). Thus, to love God is to be linked with serving the Lord, with building a community of justice and compassion (Deut 11:13). In return, God promises they will be well looked after (Deut 11:15). However, the Lord warns about letting their hearts be seduced by the gods of wealth and power (Deut 11:16).[19] If they are seduced into exploiting the poor politically or economically, marginalizing widows, orphans, or immigrants (who were especially vulnerable because of their lack of protection within the community), then attempts to worship God will be hypocritical and Israel will be punished (Amos 8:4-6).[20]

The prophets unequivocally condemn the ruthless oppression of the poor: "Ah, you who make iniquitous decrees, who write oppressive statutes, to turn aside the needy from justice..." (Isaiah 10:1). Amos scathingly decries the Israelites when they "oppress the poor, [and] crush the needy" (Amos 4:1); Ezekiel denounces the rich for their "banditry" against the poor (Ezekiel 22:29); Isaiah, their land grabbing (Isaiah 5:8); and Jeremiah, their abuse of power (Jeremiah 22:13-17). The Lord will love the wealthy *only* when they are acting justly and using their power in solidarity with the poor. They could pray with beautiful rituals, even claiming to be poor in spirit and utterly dependent on God, but the Lord will ignore them until such time as they act justly towards the defenseless: "Look, you fast only to quarrel and to fight and to strike with a wicked fist. Such fasting as you do today will not make your voice heard on high. Is such the fast that I choose, a day to humble oneself? Is it to bow down the head like a bulrush, and to lie in sackcloth and ashes? Will you call this a fast, a day acceptable to the Lord?" (Isaiah 58:4-5). The worship that pleases God must be a search for justice and a turning to the marginalized and oppressed (Isaiah 1:10-17; 58:6-7). The mission of the Messiah subsequently will be to defend the rights of the defenseless (Isaiah 11:4; Psalm 72:2-4); and this, indeed, is what Jesus did.

In his teaching and life-style, Jesus proclaimed that the poor who have been marginalized by the bullying power of the wealthy are to be privileged "heirs of the kingdom" (James 2:5). He is the Messiah of the poor: "The Spirit of the Lord ... has anointed me ... to let the oppressed go free" (Luke 4:18). After an ambivalent reaction on the part of his listeners (Luke 4:22), Jesus reiterated by way of examples from the lives of the prophets Elijah and Elisha (Luke 4:24-27) that his mission is preferentially directed towards the underprivileged and marginalized. He maintained this theme in all his preaching.

Though God had stood beside the victims of violence before Jesus' coming, in Jesus there is obvious *total* identification with the exploited. Jesus himself is the poor one, born in a stable (Luke 2:7), the vulnerable one who is killed in the service of the powerless (Luke 23:35).

In Matthew's text of the Beatitudes, Jesus speaks of two groups of people especially loved by God. First, the poor of the land, the *anawim*. Their attitudes and lifestyles are contrary to the culture around them. For them wealth, power, and selfishness have nothing to do with happiness which is to be found only in the reign of God and in God's righteousness. The second group includes those advocates who stand up to protect the rights of the powerless and who, by suppressing self-love and ambition, show mercy.

They struggle to develop peace in an unjust society and are prepared to suffer for the defense of justice: "for theirs is the kingdom of heaven" (Matthew 5:3). The *evangelically poor* belong to the *anawim*. They are people with wealth and power but without undue love of such gifts. They offer themselves and their gifts for the service of God, their sisters and brothers; they seek to build solidarity with the poor and powerless and may even identify with them, sometimes in radical ways, just as Jesus did.[21]

In contrast to the Gospel of Matthew, in which the "poor" are generally referred to *metaphorically*, Jesus in the Gospel of Luke speaks of the *materially* poor: "Blessed are you who are poor" (Luke 6:20), "But woe to you who are rich" (Luke 6:24).[22] The poor are the economically and socially powerless — primarily widows, orphans, lepers, and strangers (refugees, sojourners, migrants). The rich must use their resources to build a just community.

These verses of the Beatitudes do not praise the lack of money or condemn people who have it. They address rather, as in the Old Testament, the gap between rich and poor that renders the poor defenseless. The rich, because their power lies in their wealth, are challenged to renounce a significant amount and to undertake unpalatable deeds, such as offering risky loans (Luke 6:35) and cancelling debts (Luke 6:37).[23] Zacchaeus, the chief tax-collector of Jericho, is praised by Jesus for giving up half his possessions to the poor following his conversion, but he still remains a wealthy man (Luke 19:1-10).[24]

In the Gospel of Luke, Jesus says more bluntly than he does in the Gospel of Matthew that the chasm between rich and poor cannot be justified; in the reign of God there will be an economic reversal.[25] Hence, the poor are called blessed, not because their poverty is something good in itself but because when the kingdom takes shape, they will be preferential beneficiaries of the change.

In the Gospel of Matthew, in Jesus' last speech prior to his crucifixion, he says unambiguously that the ultimate indication of social good health is whether or not a community is committed to justice, especially to overturning the violence that renders people powerless, hungry, deprived, or otherwise oppressed. Jesus so identifies with the defenseless that when people refuse them justice they are effectively refusing *him* justice, even if they are unconscious of this (Matthew 25:40, 45).

In brief, Jesus describes a key sign of the reign of God: those who are powerless are to be the first. There are five parables in Luke's Gospel which are stories of social, economic, and political reversal in which marginalized people are described as being right before God — not necessarily because they are good but because they are, in their various ways, aware of their sinfulness and turn from it. Such persons will be given preferential status in the kingdom of God and are illustrated by the Samaritan, but not the status-proud priests and Levites (Luke 10:29-37); Lazarus, but not the wealthy rich man (Luke 16:19-31); the tax collector, but not the Pharisee (Luke 18:9-14); the last-seated at a banquet, but not the rich invited ones (Luke 14:15-24); and the prodigal son, but not his envious and self-righteous brother (Luke 15:11-32).[26]

Finally, the Letter of James provides a case study of the evil of bullying the poor by focusing on the rights of employees at harvest time. The study is important for two reasons: firstly, the language used to condemn the selfish rich is very harsh and uncompromising and secondly, it emphasizes the *powerlessness* of bullied people. "Listen! The wages of the laborers who mowed your fields, which you kept back by fraud, cry out, and the cries of the harvesters have reached the ears of the Lord of hosts. You have lived on the earth in luxury ... You have condemned and murdered the righteous one, who does not resist you" (James 5:4-6). Strong words, but the message is clear: injustice is murder; the oppressor is a murderer.[27]

Principle 4. Foster the values and structures of openness in organizations and clearly state that bullying is to have no place in them.

As we have seen, organizations can be divided into two broad kinds, that is, closed and open.[28] In an open organization, leaders deliberately encourage mutuality and dialogue at all levels and in this atmosphere, bullies find little or no support. Accountability and transparency are encouraged throughout the organization. South Africa's Truth and Reconciliation Commission that was established after the collapse of apartheid is an example of an attempt to establish an open society to replace a culture of bullying.[29]

Closed organizations, by contrast, are hierarchical and inherently foster bullying. Their leaders assume they know everything necessary for the organization and decisions are made by the top officials, are declared to be final and are communicated from the top, downwards. Leaders understand their task to be maintaining the status quo, discouraging any initiative or experimentation by people other than themselves. Subordinates obey for fear of losing their jobs or being excluded from the group in various ways. Closed systems however cannot be justified by the gospel. Any demand for blind and unquestioning obedience can never be a virtue since it denies the basic human right to be heard in whatever pertains to one's destiny.[30]

Example: should the Church be an open or a closed culture?

If the Church were to become a closed culture, writes theologian Karl Rahner, it would turn itself into "an absolute monarchy or totalitarian system," that is, a culture of bullying.[31] The Spirit does not work through only official ecclesiastical authorities; and both institutional and prophetic structures will not function as the Spirit wishes unless there are people at *all* levels of the Church's life striving to foster a spirit of mutuality or interdependence, patience, respect, and charity. Only when there is such a spirit of mutuality will the Church be and remain a truly open system or culture as desired and practiced by its founder.

Principle 5: Identify and challenge prejudices within oneself, one's workplace, and one's community because prejudices lie at the root of bullying.

Jesus was acutely aware of the prejudices and discriminatory behavior of the people of his time and place and actively sought to counter them. Moreover, he did this through his telling of parables as well as his actions. Hence, he challenged people to accept Samaritans, to associate with marginalized Jews as well as the elite, to respect women, and to forgive enemies.[32]

• *Accepting Samaritans.* Jews looked on Samaritans in a racist manner, considering them to be heretical, stupid, and lazy — but the Samaritans also had similar views of their Jewish neighbors. Scripture scholar John McKenzie points out that "there was no deeper break of human relations in the contemporary world than the feud of Jews and Samaritans, and the breadth and depth of Jesus' doctrine of love could demand no greater act of a Jew than to accept a Samaritan as a brother."[33] Hence, when Jesus told the story of the Good Samaritan (Luke 10:29-37), his listeners would have been left in no doubt about its meaning for them... A man is left to die on the roadside. Some very important people in the Jewish hierarchy see him dying but excuse themselves from any obligation to come to his assistance because they are preoccupied by other concerns. However, one person considered by the Jewish people to be stupid and uncouth — a Samaritan — sees the dying Jew and immediately goes to his aid. Jesus' listeners must have been stunned not just to have been told the story but to have been told after its conclusion: "Go and do likewise" (Luke 10:37). They could not be his followers and at the same time hold on to ethnic or racist prejudices. Jesus could not have contrasted these two incompatible ways of being more dramatical.

• *Associating with the marginalized.* Unlike the Pharisees, Jesus associates with sinners, that is, those who are known to be violators of the Jewish moral and ritual code: "Now all the tax collectors and sinners were coming near to listen to him. And the Pharisees and the scribes were grumbling and saying, 'This fellow welcomes sinners and eats with them' " (Luke 15:1-2).

• *Dialoguing with the elite.* While strongly disagreeing with the scribes and Pharisees, Jesus nonetheless acts without prejudice towards them in a spirit of dialogue and openness. We even see him dining at the house of a Pharisee, overlooking the fact that his host had failed to show him the customary welcome. Jesus instead uses the occasion to point out gently what true conversion means by reflecting on the deep repentance and love of the woman who washed his feet with her tears and "wiped them away with her hair" (Luke 7:44).

• *Respecting women.* According to Jewish culture at the time of Jesus, women were considered inferior to men. They were excluded from the worship and teaching of God and had little status beyond that of slaves. Jesus, however, acted towards them in countercultural ways. He taught women (Luke 10:38-42), gave them a rank equal with men as descendants of Abraham (Luke 13:10-17), afforded them the highest respect as persons (Matthew 5:28), and brought them into his inner circle of friends (Luke 8:1-3).[34] Finally, he appeared to Mary Magdalene before the apostles, charging her to carry the news of his resurrection to them (John 20:11-18).

• *Forgiving enemies.* As the Father is prepared to forgive, so Jesus instructs his followers that they must forgive one another (Matthew 6:14; Luke 17:3-4). Jesus sets the ultimate example by forgiving his executioners (Luke 23:34).

THIRTEEN PRACTICAL SUGGESTIONS FOR OVERCOMING PREJUDICE AND DISCRIMINATION

Prejudice is commonly thought to precede and be the cause of discrimination, but discrimination may also precede prejudice and be a cause of it. Moreover, because prejudice and discrimination feed on each other, both evils should be dealt with simultaneously along the lines of the following suggestions.

1. Seek self-knowledge

"I am," writes Charles Lamb, the English essayist (1775–1834), "in plainer words, a bundle of prejudices — made up of likings and dislikings." He speaks for all of us. If we are blinded by prejudice, we fail to see the rich insights or sufferings of others and even the causes around us for joy. And as prejudice is often the cause of bullying, there is a need to be vigilant about one's own feelings and actions. Paulo Freire, the Brazilian educator (1921–1997), warns the violated not to adopt the prejudices and behavior of the oppressor in self-defense: "the oppressed must not, in seeking to regain their humanity ... become in turn oppressors of the oppressors, but rather the restorers of the humanity of both."[35]

St. Augustine prayed: "That I may know myself, that I may know Thee, O Lord." We can extend this prayer to: "That I may know my prejudices — all that blinds me to seeing You in others, for then I will know You better." Knowledge of oneself demands change in oneself. Anyone wishing to help others must first be prepared to undertake thorough analysis of their own prejudices. The blind cannot lead the blind.

The battle against prejudice is firstly a call to one's own conversion and to justice and love in the Lord, before being a call to others' conversion. Recall that racial or cultural intolerance does not rest always on ignorance but on the desire to manipulate or control people to one's advantage. Sometimes, the mere knowledge of how prejudice works in and through oneself will do nothing to destroy it: one must be motivated to abandon prejudice within oneself as well as within one's own culture.

When reflecting on one's own prejudices or in helping others such as members of Christian study groups to become sensitive to the power of prejudice in their own lives, it is wise to begin gatherings in an atmosphere of prayer. We can do this by, for example, recalling how Jesus countered prejudice. (We saw several examples of this earlier, under Principle 5.) Then, it is beneficial to encourage prayer for conversion to truth and release from the grip of prejudice.

2. Educate others about bullying being a public health problem[36]

Bullying in its various forms is a social disease which, if improperly treated, will lead to more violence against innocent people. As punishment alone is rarely the best response to it, it is desirable to foster public educational programs to alert people to its causes and evil effects. Voluntary agencies such as the churches, sports clubs, and trade unions can have a key role in developing and supporting such programs. If governments and these agencies are not up-front in condemning any form of bullying behavior, they are sending the clear message that intimidation is permissible.

Terrorism is unacceptable in any circumstances. However, it may arise in response to society's neglect of injustices experienced by terrorists or the people they claim to represent. Hence, an important way of preventing terrorism is to remove injustices or prevent them developing.

3. Avoid ethnic jokes

Ethnic jokes are common in most societies but are they really funny? Reflect on the following:

> How do you make an Irishman laugh on Monday?
> Tell him a joke on Friday!

On careful examination, we can see that the object of an ethnic joke like this one is to "put down" members of a certain group while, at the same time, implicitly presenting one's own group as superior. Ethnic jokes are unjust and can be painful to members of target groups, who, if they are present when the jokes are told, may be expected to laugh and accept their humiliation.

Sometimes one hears the defensive comment: "I know members of minority groups who really enjoy the jokes and they even retell them to one another. So why all the fuss about such jokes?" When minority members retell ethnic jokes degrading themselves, they do so frequently to deprive the jokes of their emotional power. By retelling them, they hope to become immune to their inherent prejudices, thus curbing their resentment towards members of the bullying culture.

4. Avoid racist and sexist language

Derogatory language involves not only humiliating jokes about other ethnic or minority groups but also the use of emotion-charged words. For example in North America, many people of Anglo-Saxon ethnicity refer to African Americans as "spades," "niggers," or "jungle bunnies," all of which are terms implying inferiority.

In Australia in the past, words like "half-caste" have been used of Aboriginal peoples. Such words must also be avoided because their connotations are racist. Aboriginal blood was thought to be undesirable and "the percentage of it in a person was calculated to determine appropriate policy towards her/him."[37] In parts of Australia, for example, it was thought desirable until quite recently to isolate people with less than 50 percent "Aboriginal blood" from other Aboriginal people in order to ensure that they became "more white." Today in Australia, we hear the expression "part-Asian" applied to migrants and their descendants. Again, there is at least unconscious racism in the expression because it is assumed that some "good white blood" has at last begun to "enter minority groups."[38]

The same warning can be given about sexist language. Male-centered cultures contain words that assume and reinforce an inferior status for women and we can use these words without realizing their offensive or unjust connotations. For example, terms like "mankind" and "chairman" can exclude women and help to perpetuate male-led cultures of domination.

5. Be critical of prejudices in the mass media

Television programs and newspapers commonly articulate and reinforce a culture's prejudices about minority groups. For example, studies of newspaper reporting in New Zealand found that headlines often identified Maori criminal offenders as Maori but rarely identified New Zealanders of Anglo-Saxon ethnicity as Anglo-Saxon.[39] When you see a prejudicial bias against minority groups in the mass media, point this out to your friends or complain to the editors of papers or both.

Following terrorist attacks in the West by members of fundamentalist Islamic groups, we need to be alert to any

A Gospel Response ❖ 115

tendencies by community leaders and the mass media (and educational texts) to brand all Muslims either directly or indirectly as terrorists.

6. Be critical of rhetoric claiming to be against violence

Politicians claim to be reducing violence or the culture of bullying under the slogan of being "tough on crime and tough on criminals." At the same time, such rhetoric can encourage people to request guns be made more freely available. This is the case in the United States where seventy million gun owners own 200,000,000 guns and where, in 1990, 64 percent of the twenty thousand people murdered were shot. Most victims knew their attacker: guns which had been bought to deter burglars were often fired at husbands, wives, and lovers.[40] The message to the wider society is an evil one: violence is to be controlled by violence, including retribution and punishment. However, a main precondition for preventing violence is neither of these alternatives but rehabilitation.[41]

*7. Acknowledge prejudice and discrimination
in our national and Church histories*

Denial is a defense mechanism for coping with guilt, anxiety, and other disturbing emotions. The unconscious erects barriers that prevent the acknowledgment of reality. People will even lie to maintain their state of denial, though they may be unaware that they are doing this. It is not only an individual way of reacting: institutions such as governments, political parties, religions, armies, and police fall into the same trap. Sociologist Stanley Cohen comments:

> Such collective denial results from professional ethics, traditions of loyalty and secrecy, mutual reciprocity or codes of silence. Myths are maintained that prevent outsiders knowing about discreditable information; there

are unspoken arrangements for concerted or strategic ignorance.[42]

Many countries including democracies such as Canada, Australia, United States, and New Zealand have developed through the cruel oppression of indigenous and minority groups.[43] Attempts to conceal these events and their tragic consequences continue to this day. People who dare to expose the denial invariably risk the wrath of those who stand to gain by remaining silent. For example, those who have uncovered the genocidal actions of past governments in Australia have been roundly condemned by politicians and others.[44] Yet the truth must be told, otherwise injustices will continue against minority groups in the future. The former Governor-General of Australia, Sir William Deane, condemned this historical amnesia:

> The starting point of Aboriginal reconciliation must be national acknowledgement of the past and of the effects of past injustice and oppression on the present and the future ... An unambiguous national apology to Australia's indigenous peoples for all the injustices of the past will of itself be a significant step towards true national reconciliation...[45]

The churches also have a serious moral obligation to challenge the nation and its institutions to overcome their historical amnesia but it would be hypocritical of them to do so without acknowledging their own lies.

Apology for abuses: John Paul II

Pope John Paul II has apologized for the wrongs committed by Catholics through history in the name of their faith,[46] for example, injustices towards indigenous peoples, Jews, Protestants, women, Muslims. Acknowledging and apologizing for sexual abuse by some clergy and religious in Australia, New Zealand, and the South Pacific Islands, the Pope wrote: "The Synod Fathers [who met in Rome in

1998] wished to apologize unreservedly to the victims for the pain and disillusionment caused to them." He then refers to the need to stop the long concealment of this tragic form of bullying within the Church: "The Church in Oceania is seeking open and just procedures to respond to complaints in this area, and is unequivocally committed to compassionate and effective care of the victims, their families, the whole community, and the offenders themselves."[47]

Encouraged by apologies of this kind, Catholics should feel empowered to call for effective equality of the sexes in the Catholic Church.[48] The maintenance of inappropriate male-centered language in the Church's public prayer is unacceptable. Rosemary Chinnici, a theologian at Berkeley (U.S.A.) complains that "traditionally, the interpretation of theology has been left to men. It is men's voices we have heard explaining images of God, telling us how to pray, deciding the relationship between Jesus and women."[49] She is correct. It is time for the particular gifts of women to be recognized, acknowledged, and affirmed in theology and ritual. "Women," writes Scripture scholar Sandra Schneiders, "do not seek to participate as imitation males or on male terms in a male construction of reality."[50]

8. Prevent bullying in schools

Research shows that children who bully are very likely to become abusive as adults.[51] At the same time, there is significant evidence that the major roots of bullying are to be found not in the school but in the homes of the perpetrators, where "aggression is learned and honed by deviousness into bullying."[52] Children who are parented in firm yet democratic ways tend to develop moral reasoning ability and socially acceptable behaviors. On the other hand, parents who are authoritarian yet permissive lay the foundations for their children to learn bullying ways.[53]

A study of bullying in Australian schools found that 20 percent of males and 18 percent of females in the age range of eight to seventeen years claimed they had been bullied weekly, with the rate showing a significant rise at the time students enter secondary school.[54] When bullying is discovered in a school, a rapid appropriate response is necessary otherwise the perpetrator will assume their behavior is acceptable. Teachers hence need to remind the bully calmly that bullying will not be tolerated, and they need also to reassure victims that action is being taken to prevent further abuse. In the longer term, effective strategies are needed by teachers (perhaps with the help of educational psychologists) to deal with the roots of bullying. This may involve helping parents to adopt more positive parenting practices, building up the self-confidence of the victim and, where necessary, that of the bully too.[55] Sadly, where the main roots of bullying are in the home, there is a very limited amount teachers or others at the school can do.[56]

9. Avoid violent entertainment

Debate continues over the influence of television and films on the development of violent attitudes and behavior. Recent research in the United States concludes however that there are three primary effects of viewing televised violence, namely: the learning of aggressive attitudes and behaviors; desensitization to violence; and the development of a fear of being victimized.[57] Supervision of children in their access to television and other media is therefore highly desirable.

10. Foster qualities of servant-leadership

Healthy groups have a clarity of task or mission, open discussions, and an environment that fosters creativity. No one individual or subgroup holds coercive power over the others and leaders call the group as a whole always to take their mission into account. Such groups adhere to a culture of servanthood that is built on a continuous two-way process: servant-leaders expect to receive honest feedback as well as to offer it to those whom they serve. This nurtures trust so people can grow and become creative. In such cultures, leaders act collaboratively with others, using their power to *enable* others to be creative rather than acting in a dominating fashion, using power *over* others to control and thwart them.

Those in positions of authority in institutions have the obligation to provide a safe environment for their staff.[58] They must inform any bullies in their organization that their behavior cannot be tolerated; failure to reform may result in dismissal.

Close-up: bullying by a high ranking staff member

In a particular hospital, a doctor had been bullying nurses for years. Administrators hesitated to do anything about this for fear that the doctor would move elsewhere, taking the custom of many patients with him. The ongoing bullying had demoralized the staff. When a new CEO was appointed, however, the staff reported that the doctor had again bullied two nurses by speaking in overly demanding and abusive ways to them. The CEO called a meeting of the managers and told them that the doctor would be immediately reprimanded and that bullying would never again be tolerated. The doctor was informed that such behavior was not to be repeated and the morale of the staff improved from that moment.

Jesus taught servant-leadership by word and example: "You know that among the Gentiles those whom they recognize as their rulers lord it over them, and their great ones are tyrants over them. But it is not [to be] so among you" (Mark 10:42-43). Jesus, by washing the feet of his disciples — something that a leader would never have done in traditional Jewish culture, reiterated that authority and power must be exercised in a collaborative way, not in a bullying manner as was customary among religious and secular officials of his time. Authority and power must be at the service of building community. Jesus' style of leadership, he insists, requires inner conversion. Without this conversion it is not possible to surrender undue control, to listen to others, and to be changed by them as well as to lead them.

Servant-leadership in the Church requires that there be a collaborative form of government. At the Second Vatican Council, there was a profound shift in the Catholic Church's understanding of itself as Church — from an emphasis on the visible institution defined by clerical authority, for example, pope, bishops, and priests, to that of the People of God, or the Pilgrim Church, in which members are bound together in a common goal of seeking to build the kingdom of God.[59] All the baptized have roles to live out but, primarily, all are sinful pilgrims searching together for salvation. All pilgrims — clergy and laity — are called first to be listeners of the Word together: "communion is the central and fundamental idea of the council's documents."[60] The Spirit belongs to the whole People of God and thus is active both through the laity and the hierarchy, "that is, [the Spirit] teaches both from the bottom up and from the top down."[61] Servant-leadership, as an integral quality of this model of Church, calls for wide accountability and inter-dependence, that is, "participation and coresponsibility at all levels [of the Church's government]."[62] Clericalism and resto-rationism are contrary to this model of Church: they constitute bullying cultures. In brief, as long as the hierarchical model of the Church continues to be over-emphasized the abuse of power will continue.[63]

11. Enact anti-bullying codes of conduct

Both secular and explicitly religious organizations need to enact codes of conduct that spell out clearly that bullying behavior is not to be tolerated and that workers have the right to protection from it. This is an act of servant-leadership.

12. Promote palliative care for the incurably, terminally ill

As explained in the previous chapter, when Western medicine focuses on the medical model, it loses its caring touch. This can be evident particularly in our approach to the dying. They can find themselves to be unwelcome anomalies in a system of high technology medicine which has developed in search of cures. The contemporary hospice or palliative care movement is a reaction against this depersonalization of the dying. At the heart of the movement is a philosophy that embraces a network of values and attitudes that tries to lessen the indignities of dying so as to maximize the human life potential of the dying and their families.[64]

13. Be alert to the onset of compassion fatigue

Media personnel will often give greater prominence to those events where their own country's political, cultural, or commercial connections are evident. They prefer to cover issues that they believe will appeal to the enjoyment of their readers and listeners, knowing that an abundance of reports on other, more disturbing realities can lead to boredom and denial, if not compassion fatigue.[65] Compassion fatigue refers to the reduction in people's capacity to feel with others in their pain and to strive to help them, as a result of overly frequent exposure to reports of bad news. The realities and unjust consequences of violence, including cultures of bullying, are conveniently avoided. For example, the media in Australia rarely highlight, in a consistent way, the injustices perpetrated against Aboriginal people and asylum seekers living in prison-like conditions.

Five practical ways victims may respond to bullying

There are five positive steps that victims of bullying can take to help overcome its demoralizing and even devastating effects. These include responding to it nonviolently; seeking help, including professional counseling; knowing one's legal rights; using humor as a form of resistance; and, ultimately, forgiving bullies.

1. Respond nonviolently

Jesus quotes the universal guideline for relating to others: "In everything do to others as you would have them do to you" (Matthew 7:12), but he extends the guideline: "But I say to you, Love your enemies and pray for those who persecute you" (Matthew 5:44). Love for one's persecutors, not the "eye for an eye" directive of the Jewish culture of old, is to be the principle of action: "You have heard that it was said, 'An eye for an eye and a tooth for a tooth.' But I say to you, Do not resist an evildoer" (Matthew 5:38-39).

Jesus is quick to explain that "no resistance" is not synonymous with accepting powerlessness or being passive in the presence of violence. The violator wants the violated to agree that they are powerless, insignificant, inferior. To be in control of one's life is a fundamental right of every person, for it is the source of one's self-esteem and the foundation of the belief that one has significance.[66] Jesus so insists on this right that he refers to common experiences of his time and place to explain what he means. Scripture scholar Walter Wink explains how Jesus says to his listeners that nonviolence does not mean passivity but claiming one's right to respect through nonviolent means.[67] Faulty interpretation of Jesus' examples has wrongly encouraged people to be passive in the presence of violence. Hence, while a Roman soldier could by law bully others to carry his baggage a limited distance only, if a person offered to carry it an extra mile, this placed the soldier in the embarrassing situation of violating Roman practice. In the light of this knowledge, Jesus says to victims of bullying: "And if anyone forces you to go one mile, go also the second mile" (Matthew 5:41). In other words, let the violator know you are not being a passive recipient of abuse.

In brief, do not remain passive when confronted with a bully. Instead, find some nonviolent way to reassert your dignity — which may mean doing things that will embarrass the bully. This though is not an act of revenge but one of self-defense. One who acts in self-defense aims to *protect* themself from injury but in revenge or retaliation a person acts after he or she has been ill-treated in an effort to *harm* the violator.[68]

2. Seek help

It is difficult, if not impossible, to dialogue with a bully through logical arguments, no matter how well you may be prepared. Harassment is not a rational process; it is rooted in the inner inadequacies of the bully and may be supported by a dysfunctional culture. Therefore, it is unwise to meet with a bully alone: positive discussion will rarely prevail in such an encounter because the bully will relish the chance to dominate the interaction. Instead, keep exact information about times and places in which bullying takes place and use this at the appropriate time in interviews you may have with others whom you may seek out for help. Indeed, seeking the help of a friend to talk over what is happening will often help you to maintain objectivity.

Example: sexual bullying at work

Mary worked in a business where most of the employees were male. A manager began to make frequent veiled sexual comments about her appearance in the presence of other male workers but Mary felt powerless to stop him. Finally, she sought a legal advisor who explained her rights to her so that she could defend herself against sexual bullying. The advisor gave her a pamphlet detailing these rights and one day she left the leaflet on the offending manager's desk in a prominent position. The bullying stopped.[69]

Changing a bully's ways necessitates an inner conversion on the bully's part and a cultural shift toward the servant model of leadership at the workplace. Culture change by one individual is difficult at any time, but it is even more difficult if the prevailing workplace culture encourages bullying. Be wary of any sudden "conversion" by a bully as it may be only temporary and manipulative. Wait for significant evidence of conversion.

If one *must* meet alone with a bully, however, one should do so as calmly as possible. Since it may be very difficult to remain in control of one's feelings, it is wise to prepare with professional advice (see below). When a bully is challenged, he or she will become more enraged and vindictive and if the victim loses his or her temper, this stirs the bully up even more — in fact, it is just what the bully wants. Violence begets violence. But one way to disarm a bully is through nonviolence, as Paul advises: act with "patience ... gentleness, and self-control" (Galatians 5:22-23). Sometimes, however, it may be necessary for a victim to seek employment elsewhere before their health breaks: some bullying situations never change and the most constructive thing that a victim can do is to remove themselves from the bully's environment.

PROFESSIONAL COUNSELING

Bullying then may cause considerable stress and victims or their friends may be unable to cope constructively with the pressures without permanently separating the victim from the bully. Without separation, victims can become increasingly paralyzed, making it impossible for them to make the right decisions about what must be done to stop the intimidation. In such cases it is essential to seek professional help. Often at the workplace, employers suggest procedures for victims to follow when making complaints and they may also provide trained counselors. However, such counselors, as employees of the same organization, are sometimes more concerned to protect their employers. When this happens, victims will need to go outside their organization for redress and protection.[70] For this reason they need to know their rights as citizens, rights which are protected by laws.

3. Know your legal rights

Democracies such as those in Britain, United States, New Zealand, and Canada have detailed legislation to protect victims of bullying, for example, at the workplace and in domestic relationships. In Australia, the various states have an *Equal Opportunity Act* which, along with its Commonwealth counterparts such as the *Race Discrimination Act* and the *Disability Discrimination Act* makes it unlawful to treat any employee less favorably on the grounds of pregnancy or disability or their age, sex, race, or ethnic background, sexual orientation, or marital status. Where bullying based on such grounds occurs, this legislation is breached. Legal action can then be taken in support of the victim — and not only against the bully but also against an employer who has not taken reasonable action to stop it.

In South Australia, the *Occupational Health, Safety and Welfare Act (1986)* is a particularly effective, successful method of stopping workplace bullying there. The *Act* defines anything that affects the employee's well-being at work as an occupational health and safety issue. Since bullying affects an employee's well-being, whatever the legislation says on occupational health and safety and risks to health also applies to workplace bullying.[71] In Canada, the different forms of bullying commonly come within one or more of the following categories of the *Criminal Code*: "uttering threats," "assault," and "aggravated assault." All these offences are punishable by the court of law.[72]

Victims, however, may be unaware of the extent of their legal rights. For this reason they need to be encouraged to seek the advice of their trade unions or legal experts. In many countries, the office of the Ombudsman may offer advice to victims about how best to proceed legally against bullies. In Britain, the Parliamentary Ombudsman deals with complaints from members of the public about injustices suffered as a result of maladministration, including bullying by the officers of government departments or other public bodies. Complaints are recorded confidentially and there is no charge for services provided by the Department of the Parliamentary Ombudsman.

Many churches have also in recent times established their own principles and procedures to respond justly and compassionately to complaints of abuse made against their ministers.[73]

4. Use humor as a form of resistance

One important way to maintain self-respect in a bullying atmosphere is through humor. Humor is the *sense* within us which sets up a kindly contemplation of the incongruities of life, and the *expression* of them in speech, literature, or other forms of art. Incongruity is at the heart of all humor. In a humorus situation, or joke, the unreal seems real for a fleeting moment, for example, animals are pictured as talking, and we are amused at the incongruity of the situation. Philosopher Henri Bergson concludes that humor aims at breaking down pomposity and arrogance. The self-important duchess who slips on the banana skin is shown to be subject to the human "law" of the unpredictable.[74] Both Bergson and the psychoanalyst Sigmund Freud agree that humor subverts the status quo because it is an attack on the predictable and on control. Through it, the freedom of the human person is exalted. Humor is a means of distancing the unpleasant, predictable — even hurtful — parts of our experience from our "real selves," by regarding them with less seriousness.[75]

When we use humor as a form of resistance we mean, therefore, that people create jokes in which the stupidity and arrogance of the oppressor are highlighted as incongruous, something humanly ridiculous. Note though that such humor is kindly because it is not intended to be directed at the bully as a *person* but at their *behavior* as a violator. In focusing on the bully's behavior, victims are able to reinforce their own sense of unity and restore the feeling of human worth.[76]

Example: humor used to undermine pomposity

A CEO of a large organization began to bully several of his managers by constantly reminding them of his superior status. He would frequently write letters to them in which he would write such comments as "I, the CEO, have the authority in this business." Everyone knew he had this authority but, by constantly insisting on it in word and print, he was reminding his managers that dissent was not possible — blind acceptance of his decisions was a requirement of employment. The managers coped with the situation by referring to him as "Mr. Authority"; whenever anyone used this title, all around would burst into loud laughter. That made them feel good and helped to put things into perspective.

There are examples in the Gospels of Jesus using such humor. His listeners were generally very poor people, oppressed by the wealthy. On one occasion Jesus said: "It is easier for a camel to go through the eye of a needle than for someone who is rich to enter the kingdom of God" (Mark 10:25). The incongruity of the imagery would have caused the very poor to feel better about themselves and God's love for them. Similarly, when Jesus applied the image of whitewashed tombs to hypocritical scribes and Pharisees, the people oppressed by their overemphasis on conformity to external religious rituals would have laughed and felt better (Matthew 23:27).[77]

5. Forgive bullies

The condition for obtaining God's forgiveness for our sins is our willingness to forgive those who offend us (Mark 11:25). To forgive is to let go the anger and resentment felt in response to the harm that is done. Ultimately, the test of one's love of God is one's willingness to do this (Luke 10:37; Matthew 18:33).

Forgiving a bully is humanly, extremely difficult, especially when the violator shows no remorse for their actions. Theologian Robert Schreiter helpfully explains that forgiveness is both a process and a decision.[78] An essential first part of the slow process is for the victim to acknowledge the enormity of the personal pain that the bullying has caused them. There is wisdom in the words of Shakespeare: "Give sorrow words: the grief that does not speak whispers the o'er-fraught heart, and bids it break."[79]

If a victim is unable to tell a trusted friend or therapist their experience of bullying and its ongoing impact, it will hold them back and they will be unable to move forward. There will be feelings of fear and sadness, pain from broken trust, and even hatred and desires for revenge. If there is no space for these feelings to be acknowledged, then the victim is in danger of turning into a mirror image of those who have harmed them.

A second part of the process of forgiveness is the conscious decision on the part of the victim to move forward. The victim decides not to be controlled by the events and feelings of the past but to build a new future for themselves. Forgiving does not mean condoning, excusing, or forgetting the bullying. In fact, while forgiving one's violator it may be necessary to seek compensation and the appropriate reform of the perpetrator. In brief, the past and lessons are not forgotten, but their power to hold back the victim from moving forward is removed. When this happens, the victim may be reconciled to the violator in their heart, even when the bully is refusing to apologize and compensate for the wrongs done.

John Lederach, a Mennonite Christian who has experience in peacebuilding in fractured societies, analyzes the relevance of verse 10 in Psalm 85 for our understanding of forgiveness.[80] The psalmist, Lederach explains, is describing the return of the exiled Israelites to their land and the chance for a new peace:

> Steadfast love and faithfulness will meet;
> righteousness and peace will kiss each other.

"Steadfast love" refers to *recognizing* what has happened together with its attendant pain and suffering; "faithfulness," to *letting go* of the past and *being open* to the future; "righteousness," to *searching for* individual and group *rights* to be upheld and due *compensation* to be granted; and "peace" to *establishing unity* and *solidarity* between the violated and the violators. The biblical process of forgiveness, therefore, is the ongoing struggle to keep these four qualities in balance.

Nelson Mandela accepted the challenge of forgiving his oppressors during many years of unjust imprisonment and, having learned the necessity and art of forgiving them, he led South Africa from apartheid to democracy with significant success. Without forgetting the past, he looked forward to a future for his nation based on truth, mercy, justice, and peace.

Five practical ways non-victims may assist victims

There are five positive steps that non-victims can take to help victims. These include: listening attentively, speaking up, providing a safe environment for the victim, providing space for them to process their grief, and assisting them in seeking reparation.

1. Listen attentively

Listen attentively to the victim's story. Gently encourage them to describe what has happened: they may have been so traumatized by their experience that they are wary of ever trusting anyone. Reassure them that they are safe with you and that what you discuss between yourselves will be treated as confidential, unless they give permission to treat it otherwise.

2. Speak up

Before confronting bullies, victims need to feel safe and that someone understands what is happening to them (see Psalm 27:5), so be alert to situations in which people may be being harassed and network with others to support those who are. Then, when appropriate, offer assistance to a victim to confront the evil.

To overlook bullying is to collude with it. Of course, to speak up against it, even in the Church, is to risk being targeted by a bully oneself or scapegoated by institutional authorities. However, it is a gospel imperative to avoid collusion (cf. Luke 4:18).

3. Provide a safe environment

Employers or superiors should reassure victims that they have the right to live and work in psychologically and physically safe environments and such leaders should apologize on behalf of their organization whenever bullying is discovered to have happened. If it has been public, the victim will be more reassured when there is immediate action against the bully. Such leaders should also seek professional advice about the best ways to proceed if the victim has been traumatized by the experience. In these circumstances, they should ensure that the victim has access to professional help to work through their frightening experiences.

4. Provide space to process grief

Grief, which can be experienced by organizations, cultures, or individuals, is the depression, sorrow, anger, guilt, or confusion that accompany significant loss. A person or group that is victimized experiences a loss of dignity. Unless violated individuals and cultures have space to acknowledge that loss has occurred and formally let it go, they remain haunted by or trapped in the past, unable to open themselves to new ways of thinking and acting. Rightly did Ovid claim that "suppressed grief suffocates."[81]

A violator does not want a victim to tell their story because the retelling can release grief and allow new energy to emerge. This is why the communist governments in Eastern Europe and in China would never allow people to mourn in public over the loss of political martyrs. The Australian government, by refusing to apologize to the Aboriginal people for two centuries of injustice against them is symbolically denying them the chance to grieve openly. Such a refusal amounts to a continuation of cultural bullying.

The lamentation psalms remind us of the importance of articulating and legitimizing the feelings of loss that a community or individual experiences in victimization. In

Psalm 74, for example, the poet complains bitterly of the destruction of the sacred temple by the Babylonian violators. This has left the people without an identity: "The enemy has destroyed everything in the sanctuary" (v. 3). God gets all the blame! (v. 1). And there is no indication that the situation will change: "We do not see our emblems; there is no longer any prophet, and there is no one among us who knows how long ... the foe [is] to scoff" (vv. 9-10). Devastation reigns supreme. But the poet begins to articulate a vision of hope by retelling the story of creation when God molded the world into an orderly shape out of the primeval chaos (vv. 15-17). Then, when the chosen people were threatened in the Exodus with destruction from the pursuing Egyptians, God by his power "divided the sea" (v. 13). With the temple's destruction new chaos erupts yet Israel, encouraged by the recounting of previous interventions by the Lord, becomes hopeful in grief, anticipating that God will restore order and identity to the nation: "Rise up, O God, plead your cause" (v. 22).

5. Assist in seeking reparation

Forgiveness on the part of the victim for what has occurred does not remove the bully's obligation to make reparation. Sometimes the violator is prepared to apologize but assumes that this automatically will lead to forgiveness and reconciliation with the victim and that the incident will be forgotten. No! Neither the violator nor the victim should forget what has happened because the lessons to be learned arising from bullying are invaluable for all concerned.[82] Hence, the final practical way non-victims may assist victims is to help them seek reparation.

Summary

1. Bullying is an evil because it denies others the freedom and dignity that comes from God.

2. We are called to have a preferential love for victims of violence, as Jesus did in word and action: "Now you are the body of Christ and individually members of it" (1 Corinthians 12:27); "If one member suffers, all suffer together with it" (1 Corinthians 12:26).

3. As prejudice is a catalyst for violence in individuals and in society, constant vigilance is required to identify and stop its manifestations. This means, for example, avoiding ethnic jokes and sexist expressions, condemning any bullying behavior, and developing organizations that foster collaborative leadership.

4. Victims should not be passive and accept power-lessness when bullied. Bystanders must also not be passive but courageously come to the aid of a victim. If they do not, they collude with bullies and share in their guilt. Every act of bullying that is not challenged fosters a culture in which violators have increasing power over victims.

5. Paulo Freire writes that "In order to dominate, the dominator has no choice but to deny true praxis [reflective practice] to the people, deny them the right to say their own word and think their own thoughts."[83] Bullies do not want victims to recount their story of the loss of dignity publicly; if they do, they will rediscover what dignity means and be re-energized to protest against the violence. Hence, one way of helping victims is to give them a safe environment to retell their stories of violation.

Questions

1. Psalm 30 is a lamentation hymn which describes the pain of a victim of oppression and at the same time hope in God's abiding love and help. Read it slowly, reflecting on its message.

2. St. Teresa of Avila (1515–1582), who was frequently bullied by members of her religious congregation and by Church leaders, writes: "In the face of so much [violence] it's not possible for us to sit with our hands folded."[84] What do you feel when you hear about violence in the world at large? In your city? Why does the gospel not leave us free "to sit with our hands folded"?

3. "An act of love, a voluntary taking on oneself of the pain of the world, increases the courage and love and hope of all," writes Dorothy Day (1879–1980), an American peace activist and advocate for the poor.[85] What does she mean?

Further Reading

The following *practical manuals* offer a first step towards dealing more effectively with bullying, but to understand the dynamics of bullying, more deeply, we need to delve into such books as those that are described under the heading *Cultural roots of bullying*. For it is only by continuing to relate theory to practice and practice to theory that we can hope to manage bullying ever-more effectively.

Practical Manuals

Andrea Adams. *Bullying at Work: How to Confront and Over-come It*. London: Virago Press, 1992.
• A short practical book by one of the first authors to focus on bullying in the workplace.

Ruth Hadikin and Muriel O'Driscoll. *The Bullying Culture*. Oxford: Butterworth-Heinemann, 2000.
• Exposes the bullying culture in the British National Health Service and offers practical advice to victims. Theory is illustrated throughout with cases studies that also have relevance in healthcare facilities in other countries.

Richard J. Hazler. *Breaking the Cycle of Violence: Interventions for Bullying and Victimization*. Washington, D.C.: Accelerated Development, 1996.
• Helpful for professional therapists and school teachers who are called to help bullies, their victims, and families.

Angela Ishmael. *Harassment, Bullying and Violence at Work: A Practical Guide to Combating Employee Abuse*. London: Industrial Society, 1999.
• Focuses on bullying in the workplace and outlines practical steps to combat it. Useful case studies for workshops on bullying.

Kevin E. McKenna. *A Concise Guide to Catholic Social Teaching*. Notre Dame, Ind.: Ave Maria Press, 2002.
• Summarizes the social teachings of the Catholic Church in a readable way. Clearly explains the rights of people in society and the workplace.

Gary Namie and Ruth Namie. *The Bully at Work: What You Can Do to Stop the Hurt and Reclaim Your Dignity on the Job*. Naperville, Ill.: Sourcebooks, Inc., 2000.
• Concentrates on corporate bullying, its human costs to employees, and the steps to take to counter it.

Peter Randall. *Adult Bullying: Perpetrators and Victims*. London: Routledge, 1997; and *Bullying in Adulthood: Assessing the Bullies and Their Victims*. London: Routledge, 2001.
• A widely acknowledged expert on bullying writes particularly helpfully for managers, counselors, social workers, and teachers.

Ken Rigby. *New Perspectives on Bullying*. London: Jessica Kingsley, 2002.
• Critically examines ways of tackling bully/victim problems that are helpful to professional workers, administrators, and psychologists.

Cultural Roots of Bullying

Gerald A. Arbuckle. *Violence, Society, and Church: A Cultural Approach*. Collegeville: Liturgical Press, 2004.
• Explains the cultural roots of violence with particular emphasis on the relationship between postmodernity and violence in fundamentalism, terrorism, and neo-liberalism.

Tony Coady and others. *Violence and Police Culture*. Melbourne: Melbourne University Press, 2000.
• Considers the defenders against violence — and occasional perpetrators of it, that is, the police; the cultural

roots of police-mediated abuse; and what we must do to prevent it.

David Garland. *The Culture of Control: Crime and Social Order in Contemporary Society*. Chicago: University of Chicago Press, 2001.
• Shows the significant relationship between the punitive approach in criminology and crime control and the rise of neo-liberalist economics and politics.

Nicky A. Jackson and Gisele C. Oates. *Violence in Intimate Relationships*. Woburn, Mass.: Butterworth-Heinemann, 1998.
• Discusses sociological and psychological issues in the violence which occurs in intimate relationships between women and men, within families, and within gay and lesbian relationships.

Barbara Perry. *In the Name of Hate: Understanding Hate Crimes*. London: Routledge, 2001.
• A systematic analysis of the way cultures of inequality organized around race, ethnicity, gender, and sexuality encourage hate crimes.

John Wright. *The Ethics of Economic Rationalism*. Sydney: University of New South Wales Press, 2003.
• Offers a professionally reasoned critique of economic rationalism (neo-liberalism).

Notes

Introduction

[1] Pope John XXIII, *Pacem in Terris*, 11 April 1963, paragraph 12.

[2] Pope John Paul II, "Respect for Human Rights," *The Tablet*, 2 January 1999, page 35.

[3] Quoted by S. and A. Lynd, *Nonviolence in America: A Documentary History*, Maryknoll: Orbis, 1998, page 219.

[4] For more on bullying at the workplace, see Andrea Adams' pioneering book, *Bullying at Work*, London: Virago, 1994.

[5] R. Hadikin and M. O'Driscoll quote this writer, namely P. Randall, in their work, *The Bullying Culture*, Oxford: Butterworth-Heinemann, 2000, on page 10.

[6] Peter Randall, while agreeing that bullying is significantly widespread at the workplace, explains why it is difficult to obtain accurate statistics. See his excellent analysis in his book, *Bullying in Adulthood: Assessing the Bullies and Their Victims*, Hove: Routledge, 2001, pages 7–18.

To follow up the data from Britain, see K. Healey, *Bullying and Peer Pressure*, Sydney: Spinney Press, 1998, page 30. For the data from Australia, see L. Doherty, *The Sydney Morning Herald*, 5 January 2002, page 3.

[7] John Wright, a philosophy professor at the University of Newcastle, Australia, notes that the term "economic rationalism" was formulated in Australia, but it connotes ideas that are referred to as '"neo-conservatism," "neo-liberalism," and "economic fundamentalism." "Thatcherism" in Britain and "Reaganomics" in the United States closely resemble economic rationalism. See Wright's book, *The Ethics of Economic Rationalism*, Sydney: University of New South Wales Press, 2003, pages vi–viii. See also M. Pusey, *Economic Rationalism in Canberra: A Nation-building State Changes Its Mind*, Cambridge: Cambridge University Press, 1991, and for the application of economic rationalism to healthcare in the United States, see V. Navarro (professor of health policy at Johns Hopkins University, U.S.A.), *The Politics of Health Policy: The U.S. Reforms 1980–1994*, Oxford: Blackwell, 1994, passim.

[8] Pope John XXIII, *Pacem in Terris*, paragraph 40.

[9] See the work edited by T. Coady and M. O'Keefe, *Terrorism and Justice*, Melbourne: Melbourne University Press, 2002, and also that by M. Ruthven, *A Fury of God: The Islamist Attack on America*, London: Granta, 2002.

[10] See B. Perry, *In the Name of Hate: Understanding Hate Crime*, London: Routledge, 2001, page 3.

[11] See B. Perry, *In the Name of Hate*, page 178.

[12] See the work of the investigative staff of the *Boston Globe*, "Betrayal: The Crisis in the Catholic Church," Boston: Little and Brown, 2002, on page 184.

[13] See N. Chomsky, *September 11*, Sydney: Allen and Unwin, 2002, page 79.

[14] See W. MacPherson, *The Stephen Lawrence Inquiry*, British Parliamentary Reports — Document number CM 4262-1, 1999.

[15] See P. Weller, *Don't Tell the Prime Minister*, Melbourne: Scribe Publications, 2002, pages 1–7. See also D. Marr and M. Wilkinson, *Dark Victory*, Crows Nest: Allen & Unwin, 2003, passim.

[16] From the Editorials, "Truth Pitched Overboard," *The Sydney Morning Herald*, 25 October 2002, page 12, and "Tampa and the Need for Truth," 31 October 2002, page 14. See also D. Marr and M. Wilkinson, *Dark Victory*, Sydney: Allen & Unwin, 2003, passim.

[17] See also G. Hage, *White Nation: Fantasies of White Supremacy in a Multicultural Society*, Annandale: Pluto Press, 1998, pages 105–8.

[18] See C. Miley, *The Suicidal Church: Can the Anglican Church Be Saved?* Sydney: Pluto Press, 2002.

Chapter 1

[1] From R. Hadikin, *The Bullying Culture*, Oxford: Butterworth-Heinemann, 2000, page 75.

[2] Compare F. Furedi, *Culture of Fear: Risk-Taking and the Morality of Low Expectation*, London: Cassell, 1998, pages 73–105.

[3] B. Byrne, *Bullying: A Community Approach*, Dublin: Columba Press, 1994, page 56.

[4] R. Mann, as reported in the *Sydney Morning Herald*, 23 April 1997, page 4.

[5] See the book edited by P. K. Smith, Y. Morita, and others, *The Nature of School Bullying: A Cross-National Perspective*, London: Routledge, 1999, page 1.

[6] P. Randall, *Bullying in Adulthood: Assessing the Bullies and Their Victims*, Hove: Routledge, 2001, page 7.

[7] See A. Ishmael, *Harassment, Bullying and Violence at Work*, London: Industrial Society, 1999, pages 61–2.

[8] See B. Senior, *Organisational Change*, London: Prentice Hall, 1996, pages 176–7.

[9] See R. May, *Power and Innocence: A Search for the Sources of Violence*, New York: W. W. Norton, 1972, pages 105–9.

[10] See G. A. Arbuckle, *Refounding the Church: Dissent for Leadership*, Homebush: St. Pauls Publications, 1993, page 79.

[11] See J. N. Lam's work, "Child Sexual Abuse," in the book edited by N. A. Jackson and G. C. Oates, *Violence in Intimate Relationships*, Boston: Butterworth-Heinemann, 1998, page 51.

[12] See G. Moody-Stuart, *Grand Corruption*, Oxford: Worldview Publishing, 1997, page 1.

[13] For more on the British example, see L. Baston, *Sleaze: The State of Britain*, London: Macmillan, 2000, pages 163–79. For more on the IOC example, see N. Jayawickrama's work, "Transparency International," in the book edited by A. Y. Lee-Chai and J. A. Bargh, *The Use and Abuse of Power*, Philadelphia: Psychology Press, 2001, page 281.

[14] See Jayawickrama, "Transparency International," pages 282–3.

[15] See S. Rose-Ackerman, *Corruption and Government: Causes, Consequences, and Reform*, Cambridge: Cambridge University Press, 1999.

[16] See J. R. Hall's work, "Mass Suicide and the Branch Davidians," in the book edited by D. G. Bromley and J. G. Melton, *Cults, Religion and Violence*, Cambridge: Cambridge University Press, 2002, pages 149–69.

[17] See R. P. Wolff's work, "On Violence," in the book edited by M. B. Steger and N. S. Lind, *Violence and Its Alternatives*, London: Macmillan, 1999, pages 12–22.

[18] G. Vanderhaar, *Beyond Violence*, Mystic: Twenty-Third Publications, 1998, page 32.

[19] This quotation from Nietzsche's writing is made by J. Glover, *Humanity: A Moral History of the Twentieth Century*, London: Jonathan Cape, 1999, page 15.

[20] See E. Staub, *The Roots of Evil: The Origins of Genocide and Other Group Violence*, Cambridge: Cambridge University Press, 1989, page 35.

[21] See V. Bowie's work, "Theories of Violence," in the book edited by K. Healey, *A Culture of Violence*, Sydney: Spinner Press, 1996, pages 1–2.

[22] See R. F. Baumeister, *Evil: Inside Human Violence and Cruelty*, New York: W. H. Freeman, 1996, pages 380–1.

[23] See G. A. Arbuckle, *Healthcare Ministry: Refounding the Mission in Tumultuous Times*, Collegeville: The Liturgical Press, 2000, pages 139–40.

[24] W. W. George, "Imbalance of Power," *Harvard Business Review,* July 2002, page 22.

[25] See *Bully Online,* website of the U.K. National Workplace Bullying Advice Line.

[26] B. Hoffman, *Inside Terrorism,* New York: Colombia University Press, 1998, page 43.

[27] See the *Sydney Morning Herald,* 20 September 2001, page 3.

[28] See B. Perry, *In the Name of Hate: Understanding Hate Crime,* London: Routledge, 2001, pages 174–8.

[29] See T. Gillespie's work, "Virtual Violence? Pornography and Violence Against Women on the Internet," in the book edited by J. Radford and others, *Women, Violence and Strategies for Action,* Buckingham: Open University Press, 2000, page 43.

[30] See I. L. Janis, *Groupthink,* Dallas: Houghton Mifflin, 1982, pages 7–9.

[31] See I. L. Janis, *Groupthink,* pages 14–47.

[32] See G. A. Arbuckle, *Refounding the Church: Dissent for Leadership,* Homebush: St. Pauls Publications, 1993, pages 112–3.

[33] C. Cooper, reported in the *Courier-Mail,* Brisbane, 16 February 2000, page 7.

[34] See S. Jones, *Understanding Violent Crime,* Buckingham: Open University Press, 2000, pages 68–85.

[35] To respect confidentiality, I am obliged to maintain the anonymity of this CEO.

[36] See M. Pepper's work, "Road Rage," *Internet* magazine, 9 June 1997, page 1.

[37] E. Cleaver, *Soul on Ice,* New York: Delata, 1968, page 14.

[38] See J. Hill and S. Amuwo's work, "Understanding Elder Abuse and Neglect," in the book edited by N. Jackson and G. Oates, *Violence in Intimate Relationships,* Woburn: Butterworth-Heinemann, 1998, pages 195–216.

[39] K. Legge, "Preying on Parents," in the *Australian,* 28 September 2002, page 26.

Chapter 2

[1] Aung San Suu Kyi, cited by J. Keane, "Fear and Democracy," in the work edited by K. Worcester and others, *Violence and Politics,* New York: Routledge, 2002, page 226.

[2] See M. Klein and J. Riviere, *Love, Hate and Reparation,* New York: Norton, 1964, page 13.

[3] See R. J. Hazler, *Breaking the Cycle of Violence*, Washington, D.C.: Accelerated Development, 1996, page 29.

[4] See P. Randall, *Adult Bullying: Perpetrators and Victims*, London: Routledge, 1997, pages 73–86; K Rigby and P. Slee's work, "Australia," in the book edited by P. K. Smith and others, *The Nature of School Bullying: A Cross-National Perspective*, London: Routledge, 1999, pages 324–39.

[5] See L. Wright and M. Smye, *Corporate Abuse*, London: Simon & Schuster, 1996, page 53.

[6] See D. Pepler and W. Craig, "What Should We Do About Bullying?" *Peacebuilder*, vol. 2, no. 1 (1999) page 9.

[7] See. D. Dutton, *The Abusive Personality: Violence and Control in Intimate Relationships*, New York: Guildford Press, 1998, pages 139–59.

[8] See N. Symington, *Emotion and Spirit: Questioning the Claims of Psychoanalysis and Religion*, London: Cassell, 1994, pages 118–20.

[9] See comments by S. White in her enlightening paper, "A Life Cycle Theory of Bullying: Persecutory Anxiety and a Futile Search for Recognition in the Workplace," *Socio-Analysis*, vol. 3, no. 2. (2001) page 144.

[10] E. Fromm, *The Heart of Man*, New York: Harper & Row, 1964, page 32.

[11] Fromm, *The Heart of Man*, page 291.

[12] E. Becker, *Escape from Evil*, New York: Free Press, 1975, pages 113–4.

[13] See R. F. Baumeisster, *Evil: Inside Human Violence and Cruelty*, W. H. Freeman: New York, 1999, page 149.

[14] See J. N. Lam's work, "Child Sexual Abuse," in the book edited by N. A. Jackson and G. C. Oates, *Violence in Intimate Relationships*, Boston: Butterworth-Heinemann, 1998, page 51.

[15] R. Brannon, quoted by N. S. Kimmel, "Masculinity as Homophobia," in the work edited by J. A. Kuypers, *Men and Power*, Halifax: Fernwood, 1999, page 90.

[16] See J. Hearn, *The Violences of Men*, London: Sage, 1998, pages 4–6.

[17] See B. Perry, *In the Name of Hate: Understanding Hate Crimes*, New York: Routledge, 2001, page 23.

[18] See S. Tomsen's work, "Sexual Identity and Victimhood in Gay-Hate Murder Trials," in the book edited by C. Cunneen and others, *Faces of Hate: Hate Crime in Australia*, Annandale: Hawkins Press, 1997, page 97.

[19] See P. van Reyk cited by S. Jones, *Understanding Violent Crime*, Buckingham: Open University Press, 2000, page 74.

[20] See P. Randall, *Adult Bullying: Perpetrators and Victims*, London: Routledge, 1997, pages 30–1.

[21] See K. Bjorkqvist and K. Osterman's work, "Finland," in the book edited by P. K. Smith and others, *The Nature of School Bullying*, London: Routledge, 1999, pages 58–9.

[22] Ruth Fink's report is cited in J. Beckett's work, "Aborigines, Alcohol and Assimilation" in the book edited by M. Reay, *Aborigines Now*, Sydney: Angus and Robertson, 1964, page 36.

[23] G. Allport, *The Nature of Prejudice*, New York: Doubleday, 1958, page 10.

[24] The *prejudice* of sexism though differs from the *cultural disease* of sexism which we will consider in Chapter 3.

[25] See R. Hampton, *Sentencing in a Children's Court and Labelling Theory*, Wellington: Justice Department, 1975, page 57.

[26] See P. Totaro's, "Tunnel Vision," in the *Sydney Morning Herald*, 23 September 2002, page 11.

[27] See B. Bowling, *Violent Racism: Victimization, Policing and Social Context*, Oxford: Oxford University Press, 1998, page 244.

[28] See *The Economist*, 27 February 1999, page 16.

[29] For reports about such crimes, see N. Fraser, *The Voice of Modern Hatred*, London: Picador, 2000.

[30] See S. Hillier and G. Scambler's work, "Women as Patients and Providers," in the book edited by G. Scambler, *Sociology as Applied to Medicine*, London: W. B. Saunders, 1997, pages 121–34.

[31] See M. Sargent and others, *The New Sociology for Australians*, Melbourne: Longman, 1997, pages 141–2.

[32] See B. Wearing, *Gender: The Pain and Pleasure of Difference*, Melbourne: Longman, 1996, page 77.

[33] See M. Furlong, *C of E: The State It's In*, London: Hodder & Stoughton, 2000, pages 360–3.

[34] For comments on this by D. Cozzens, see his *Sacred Silence: Denial and Crisis in the Church*, Collegeville: The Liturgical Press, 2002, pages 117–23.

[35] See C. Osiek, *Beyond Anger: On Being a Feminist in the Church*, New York: Paulist, 1986, pages 9–10.

[36] See "Changes at the Top" (anon.), and M. Taylor, "Truth, Justice and ICEL," in the *Tablet*, 17 August 2002, pages 19–21 and 26–27, respectively.

[37] See P. Randall, *Adult Bullying: Perpetrators and Victims*, London: Routledge, 1997, page 57.

[38] See Randall, *Adult Bullying*, page 49.

[39] See Randall, *Adult Bullying*, page 49.

⁴⁰ Harrison's experience is related by M. Evans, *The Times* (U.K.), 21 July 2000, page 3.

⁴¹ To protect the victim, I am obliged not to disclose her name.

⁴² Robyn Mann's research is quoted by M. Sweet, "Stress at Work: How Office Bullies Use Torture Tactics," in the *Sydney Morning Herald*, 23 April 1997, page 4.

⁴³ See E. Fromm, *The Heart of Man*, New York: Harper & Row, 1964, pages 285–7.

⁴⁴ U.S.A. Conference of Catholic Bishops, "Economic Justice for All," *Origins*, vol. 16, no. 24 (1986) page 560.

⁴⁵ To protect the executive, I am obliged not to disclose his name.

⁴⁶ See A. C. McFarlane and B. A. Van der Kolk's work, "Trauma and Its Challenge to Society," in the book edited by B. A. van der Kolk and others, *Traumatic Stress*, New York: Guilford Press, 1996, page 28.

⁴⁷ See A. C. McFarlane and B. van der Kolk, "Trauma and Its Challenge to Society," page 31.

⁴⁸ For more on PTSD, see M. Thomas and J. Pierson, *Dictionary of Social Work*, London: Collins, 1995, pages 277–9; and American Psychiatric Association, *Diagnostic and Statistical Manual of Mental Disorders*, Washington: American Psychiatric Association, 1994, pages 424–5.

⁴⁹ See P. Randall, *Bullying in Adulthood: Assessing the Bullies and Their Victims*, Hove: Routledge, 2001, pages 147–64.

⁵⁰ See J-A. O'Hagan, *Sydney Morning Herald*, 20 July 2002, page 1.

Chapter 3

¹ See E. Picard, "The Lebanese Shi'a and Political Violence in Lebanon," in the work edited by D. Apter, *The Legitimization of Violence*, London: Macmillan, 1997, page 208.

² See E. Hall, *The Silent Language*, New York: Doubleday, 1959.

³ See G. A. Arbuckle, *Earthing the Gospel: An Inculturation Handbook for Pastoral Workers*, Homebush: St. Pauls Publications, 1990, pages 29–43. See also R. May, *Power and Innocence: A Search for the Sources of Violence*, New York: W. W. Norton, 1998, pages 50–7.

⁴ See B. Kapferer, *Legends of People, Myths of State: Violence, Intolerance, and Political Culture in Sri Lanka and Australia*, Washington: Smithsonian Institution Press, 1988, pages 149–218.

⁵ See A. Ishmael, *Harassment, Bullying and Violence at Work*, London: Industrial Society, 1999, pages 131–2.

[6] See J. Bargh and J. Alvarez's work, "The Road to Hell: Good Intentions in the Face of Nonconscious Tendencies to Misuse Power," in the book edited by A. Lee-Chai and J. Bargh, *The Use and Abuse of Power*, New York: New York University, 2001, pages 41–53.

[7] See J.B.L. Chan, *Changing Police Culture: Policing in a Multicultural Society*, Cambridge: Cambridge University Press, 1997, pages 90–3. See also J. Kleinig's work, "Police Violence and the Loyal Code of Silence," in the book edited by T. Coady and others, *Violence and Police Culture*, Melbourne: Melbourne University Press, 2000, pages 219–34.

[8] See G. Morgan, *Images of Organization*, Beverly Hills: Sage, 1986, pages 210–12.

[9] See S. Brownmiller, *Against Our Will: Men, Women and Rape*, New York: Simon and Schuster, 1975; A. Dworkin, *Pornography: Men Possessing Women*, New York: G. P. Putnam, 1979; and L. Kelly and J. Radford's work, "The Problem of Men: Feminist Perspectives on Sexual Violence," in the book edited by P. Scraton, *Law, Order and the Authoritarian State*, Milton Keynes: Open University Press, 1987, pages 237–53.

[10] See A. J. Goldsmith, "An Impotent Conceit: Law, Culture and the Regulation of Police Violence," in the book edited by T. Coady and others, *Violence and Police Culture*, Melbourne: Melbourne University Press, 2000, pages 123–5.

[11] J. Glover quotes A. Eichmann in the work, *Humanity: A Moral History of the Twentieth Century*, London: Jonathan Cape, 1999, page 336.

[12] See T. Smyth, *Caring for Older People*, London: Macmillan, 1992, pages 11–45.

[13] See G. A. Arbuckle, *Grieving for Change: A Spirituality for Refounding Gospel Communities*, Homebush: St. Pauls Publications, 1991, pages 47–8.

[14] See D. Dempsey, *The Way We Die: An Investigation of Death and Dying in America*, New York: McGraw-Hill, 1975, page 81.

[15] See G. A. Arbuckle, *Refounding the Church: Dissent for Leadership*, Homebush: St. Pauls Publications, 1993, pages 82–4.

[16] See A. Dulles, *A Church to Believe In: Discipleship and the Dynamics of Freedom*, New York: Crossroad, 1982, pages 36–7.

[17] See J. Chittister, "Mary Ward: Women and Leadership," *The Way*, Summer 1985, page 59.

[18] See J. R. Saul, *Voltaire's Bastards: The Dictatorship of Reason in the West*, London: Penguin, 1992, page 106.

[19] See L. Wright and M. Smye, *Corporate Abuse*, London: Simon and Schuster, 1996, pages 77–8.

[20] See L. Wright and M. Smye, *Corporate Abuse*, page 61.

[21] Peter Saunders argues that the term "economic rationalism" gives a false impression. It wrongly conveys the idea of economic *reasoning* when in fact it is an *unproven ideology* that is chosen to motivate decision-making. See his book, *The Ends and Means of Welfare: Coping with Economic and Social Change in Australia*, Cambridge: Cambridge University Press, 2002, page 9.

[22] John R. Saul, in his Canadian Massey Lecture, comments: "[We] are deregulating everything in sight and even restructuring government and education along industry lines. We have fallen back in love with an old ideology that has never paid off in the past." (*The Unconscious Civilization*, New York: Penguin, 1995, page 122.)

[23] See L. Edwards, *How to Argue with an Economist*, Cambridge: Cambridge University Press, 2002.

[24] See *The Australian Oxford Paperback Dictionary*, edited by F. Ludowyk and B. Moore, Melbourne: Oxford University Press, 2001, page 251.

[25] See J. Mohan's work, "Privatization in the British Health Sector: A Challenge to the NHS?" in the book edited by J. Gabe and others, *The Sociology of the Health Service*, London: Routledge, 1991, page 40.

[26] See the Proceedings of the Fabian Health Association Conference, *Health Crisis — What Crisis?*, London: Fabian Society, 1996, page 2.

[27] See H. Swerissen, and S. Duckett's work, "Health Policy and Financing," in the book edited by H. Gardner, *Health Policy in Australia*, Melbourne: Oxford University Press, 1997, page 33.

[28] See G. A. Arbuckle, *Healthcare Ministry: Refounding the Mission in Tumultuous Times*, Collegeville: The Liturgical Press, 2000, pages 74–5; see also L. Edwards, *How to Argue with an Economist*, Cambridge: Cambridge University Press, 2002, pages 86–93.

[29] See P. Saunders, *The Ends and Means of Welfare: Coping with Economic and Social Change in Australia*, Cambridge: Cambridge University Press, 2002, page 250.

[30] John Howard's comments were made on a radio program hosted by John Laws and quoted in *Sydney Morning Herald*, 25 October 1996, page 1. See the book edited by C. Cunneen and others, *Faces of Hate: Hate Crime in Australia*, Sydney: Hawkins Press, 1997, page 6.

[31] See the analysis made by R. Mann, *In Denial: The Stolen Generations and the Right*, Melbourne: Black Inc., 2001.

[32] See R. Fitzpatrick's work, "Society and Changing Patterns of Disease," in the book edited by G. Scambler, *Sociology as Applied to Medicine*, London: W. B. Saunders, 1997, pages 3–30.

[33] See the analysis made by D. Garland, *The Culture of Control: Crime and Social Order in Contemporary Society*, Chicago: Chicago University Press, 2001, page 175.

[34] See the Introduction to the book edited by D. Brown and M. Wilkie, *Prisoners as Citizens: Human Rights in Australian Prisons*, Sydney: Federation Press, 2002, page xx.

[35] See E. Staub, *The Roots of Evil: The Origins of Genocide and Other Group Violence*, Cambridge: Cambridge University Press, 1989, page 48.

[36] See R. Moore, *The Formation of a Persecuting Society: Power and Deviance in Western Europe 900–1250*, Oxford: Basil Blackwell, 1987, page 98.

[37] See P. Kelly, "Hanson — Symptom of a Deeper Problem," in *Two Nations: The Causes and Effects of the Rise of the One Nation Party in Australia*, Melbourne: Bookman, 1998, pages 89–102.

[38] See P. Weller, *Don't Tell the Prime Minister*, Melbourne: Scribe Publications, 2002.

[39] See N. Abercrombie and others, *Dictionary of Sociology*, London: Penguin, 2000, page 231.

[40] See E. Goode and N. Ben-Yehuda, *Moral Panics: The Social Construction of Deviance*, Oxford: Blackwell, 1994, and G. O'Donnell, *Work Out Sociology*, London: Macmillan, 1987, page 142.

[41] This excerpt from J. H. Newman's letter to J. Keble of 6 September 1843 is cited by J. G. Faus, *Where the Spirit Breathes: Prophetic Dissent in the Church*, Maryknoll: Orbis Books, 1989, page 103.

[42] See D. McLoughlin's work, "Authority as Service," in the book edited by N. Timms and K. Wilson, *Governance and Authority in the Roman Catholic Church*, London: SPCK, 2000, page 136.

[43] See G. A. Arbuckle, *Refounding the Church: Dissent for Leadership*, Homebush: St Paul Publications, 1993, pages 15–97, and *Earthing the Gospel: An Inculturation Handbook for Pastoral Workers*, Homebush: St. Pauls Publications, 1990, pages 119–27 and 135–8.

Chapter 4

[1] Alexander Solzenitsyn, quoted by J. Glover, in *Humanity: A Moral History of the Twentieth Century*, London: Jonathan Cape, 1999, page 401.

[2] B. J. Malina and R. L. Rohrbaugh, *Social Science Commentary on the Synoptic Gospels*, Minneapolis: Fortress Press, 1989, page 215.

[3] F. E. Katz, *Ordinary People and Extraordinary Evil*, Albany: State University of New York, 1993, page 5.

4 See R. F. Baumeister, *Evil: Inside Human Violence and Cruelty*, New York: W. H. Freeman, 1999, pages 375–85.

5 See the Latin American Bishops' "Puebla Document 1979" in the book edited by J. Eagleson and P. Scharper, *Puebla and Beyond*, Maryknoll: Orbis Books, 1979, pages 183–4.

6 See G. V. Pixley's "Divine Judgment in History" in the book, *The Idols of Death and the God of Life*, edited by P. Richard and others, Maryknoll: Orbis Books, 1983, pages 46–65.

7 See John Paul II, *The Gospel of Life,* 25 March (1995) and commentary on it by M.L.H. Mich, *Catholic Social Teaching and Movements*, Mystic, Conn.: Twenty-Third Publications, 2000, pages 226–35.

8 See F. E. Katz, *Ordinary People and Extraordinary Evil*, Albany: State University of New York, 1993, page 19.

9 See H. Arendt, *Eichmann in Jerusalem: A Report on the Banality of Evil*, New York: Penguin Books, 1964, passim.

10 See Arendt, *Eichmann in Jerusalem*, page 276.

11 See F. E. Katz, *Ordinary People and Extraordinary Evil*, Albany: State University of New York, 1993, page 19.

12 See C. Browning, *Ordinary Men: Reserve Battalions 101 and the Final Solution in Poland*, New York: Aaron Asher, 1992, and Trudy Grovier, *Forgiveness and Revenge*, London: Routledge, 2002, pages 115–40.

13 See T. Merton, *Thomas Merton on Peace*, London: Mowbray, 1971, pages 82, 84.

14 See F. E. Katz, *Ordinary People and Extraordinary Evil*, Albany: State University of New York, 1993, page 13; and P. Augar, *The Death of Gentlemanly Capitalism*, London: Penguin, 2000, pages 43–173.

15 See S. McDonagh, *To Care for the Earth: A Call to a New Theology*, London: Geoffrey Chapman, 1986, page 27.

16 See M. S. Peck, *People of the Lie: The Hope for Healing Human Evil*, New York: Simon and Schuster, 1983, pages 242–3.

17 See T. Govier, *Forgiveness and Revenge*, London: Routledge, 2002, page 159.

18 See comments by B. J. Malina and R. L. Rohrbaugh, *Social Science Commentary on the Synoptic Gospels*, Minneapolis: Fortress Press, 1989, pages 315–6.

19 See D. R. Hillers, *Covenant: The History of a Biblical Idea*, Baltimore: Johns Hopkins University Press, 1969, page 152.

20 See M. Elsbernd and R. Bieringer, *When Love is Not Enough: A Theo-ethic of Justice*, Collegeville: The Liturgical Press, 2002, pages 41–6.

[21] See L. Boff and C. Boff, *Introducing Liberation Theology*, Maryknoll: Orbis Books, 1987, pages 48–9.

[22] See M. Elsbernd and R. Bieringer, *When Love Is Not Enough: A Theoethic of Justice*, Collegeville: The Liturgical Press, 2002, page 49.

[23] See D. J. Bosch, *Transforming Mission: Paradigm Shifts in Theology of Mission*, Maryknoll: Orbis Books, 1991, page 103.

[24] See R. Charles, *The Social Teaching of Vatican II*, Oxford: Platter Publications, 1982, page 302.

[25] See J. L. McKenzie, *Dictionary of the Bible*, London: Geoffrey Chapman, 1965, page 684.

[26] See G. A. Arbuckle, *Healthcare Ministry: Refounding the Mission in Tumultuous Times*, Collegeville: The Liturgical Press, 2000, pages 170–1.

[27] See Gustavo Gutierrez, *The God of Life*, Maryknoll: Orbis Books, 1988, pages 129–30.

[28] See O. G. Mink and others, *Developing and Managing Open Organizations*, Santa Barbara: Organizations and Human Resource Development, 1979, pages 3–19.

[29] See comments by R. S. Appleby, *The Ambivalence of the Sacred: Religion, violence, and reconciliation*, Lanham: Rowman and Littlefield, 2000, pages 197–204.

[30] See K. Rahner, *Theological Investigations*, vol. 12, New York: Seabury Press, 1974, pages 94–7.

[31] K. Rahner, *Theological Investigations*, vol. 12, page 89.

[32] See G. A. Arbuckle, *Earthing the Gospel: An Inculturation Handbook for Pastoral Workers*, Homebush: St. Pauls Publications, 1990, pages 158–65.

[33] J. L. McKenzie, *Dictionary of the Bible*, London: Geoffrey Chapman, 1965, page 766.

[34] See E. Achtemeier's article, "Women," in the book edited by B. Metzger and M. Coogan, *The Oxford Companion to the Bible*, New York: Oxford University Press, 1993, page 807.

[35] See P. Freire, *Pedagogy of the Oppressed*, New York: Herder and Herder, 1968, page 28.

[36] See J. Gilligan, *Preventing Violence*, London: Thames and Hudson, 2001, pages 18–28.

[37] See M. Sargent, *The New Sociology for Australians*, Melbourne: Longman, 1997, page 231; see also R. Wilson and others, *Bringing Them Home: National Enquiry into the Separation of Aboriginal and Torres Strait Islander Children from Their Families*, Sydney: Sterling Press, 1997, passim.

[38] See the helpful analysis by G. Hage, *White Nation: Fantasies of White Supremacy in a Multicultural Society*, Annandale: Pluto Press, 1998.

[39] See A. Ballara, *Proud to Be White: A Survey of Pakeha Prejudice in New Zealand*, Auckland: Heinemann, 1986, pages 143–6.

[40] See *The Economist*, 7 September 1991, page 20.

[41] See J. Gilligan, *Preventing Violence*, London: Thames and Hudson, 2001, pages 136–8.

[42] S. Cohen, *States of Denial: Knowing About Atrocities and Suffering*, Cambridge: Polity, 2001, page 6.

[43] See the work edited by P. Havemann, *Indigenous Peoples' Rights in Australia, Canada, and New Zealand*, Auckland: Oxford University Press, 1999, passim.

[44] See C. Cunneen and others, *Faces of Hate: Hate Crime in Australia*, Annandale: Hawkins Press, 1997, pages 1–14.

[45] W. Deane, reported in the *Sydney Morning Herald*, 9 November 2001, page 19.

[46] See L. Accattoli, *When a Pope Asks Forgiveness: The Mea Culpas of John Paul II*, New York: Alba House, 1998, passim.

[47] See John Paul II, *The Church in Oceania*, Sydney: St. Pauls, 2001, paragraph 49.

[48] See, for example, M. Macdonald and others, *Woman and Man: One in Christ — Report on the Participation of Women in the Catholic Church in Australia*, Sydney: HarperCollins, 1999, passim.

[49] See R. Chinnici, *Can Women Re-Image the Church?*, New York: Paulist, 1992, page 1.

[50] See S. M. Schneiders, *Beyond Patching: Faith and Feminism in the Catholic Church*, New York: Paulist, 1991, page 36.

[51] See D. Fitzgerald, *Bullying in Our Schools*, Dublin: Blackhall, 1999, page 34.

[52] See P. Randall, "Pre-School Children: Experiences of Being Parented and the Routes to Bullying," in the work edited by D. Tattum and G. Herbert, *Bullying: Home, School and Community*, London: David Fulton, 1997, page 5.

[53] See Randall, "Pre-School Children," page 5.

[54] See D. Fitzgerald, *Bullying in Our Schools*, Dublin: Blackhall, 1999, page 24; K. Rigby and P. T. Slee, "Australia," in the work edited by P. K. Smith and others, *The Nature of School Bullying: A Cross-National Perspective*, London: Routledge, 1999, pages 324–39.

[55] See D. Tattum and D. Lane, *Bullying in Schools*, Oakhill: Trentham Books, 1988, passim.

[56] See B. Byrne, *Bullying: A Community Approach*, Dublin: Columba Press, 1994, page 81.

[57] See J. Federman and others, *National Television Violence Study*, Thousand Oaks: SAGE, 1998, page 7. For comments on research in Australia, see J. Schultz in "Queens of the Screen or Princes of Media," in the work edited by J. M. Najman and J. S. Western, *A Sociology of Australian Society*, Melbourne: Macmillan, 1993, pages 603–5.

[58] See A. Adams, *Bullying at Work: How to Confront and Overcome It*, London: Virago Press, 1992, pages 167–87.

[59] See "The Church," in *The Documents of Vatican II*, edited by W. Abbott, London: Geoffrey Chapman, 1966, paragraphs 48–51.

[60] See "The Final Report" of the World Synod of Catholic Bishops, 1985, *Origins*, 19 December 1985, page 44.

[61] See T. L. Nichols, *That All May Be One: Hierarchy and Participation in the Church*, Collegeville: The Liturgical Press, 1997, page 317.

[62] See Nichols, *That All May Be One*, page 44.

[63] See G. A. Arbuckle, *Refounding the Church: Dissent for Leadership*, Sydney: St. Pauls Publications, 1993, pages 36–127.

[64] See C. Saunders, "Hospices Worldwide: A Mission Statement," in the work she edited with R. Kastenbaum, *Hospice Care on the International Scene*, New York: Springer, 1997, pages 3–12.

[65] See S. D. Moeller, *Compassion Fatigue,* New York: Routledge, 1999, pages 17–54.

[66] See R. May, *Power and Innocence: A Search for the Sources of Violence*, New York: W. W. Norton, 1988, page 243.

[67] See W. Wink, *Engaging the Powers: Discernment and Resistance in a World of Domination*, Minneapolis: Fortress Press, 1992, pages 471–6.

[68] See T. Grovier, *Forgiveness and Revenge*, London: Routledge, 2002, page 2.

[69] A similar incident is reported by A. Ishmael, *Harassment, Bullying and Violence at the Workplace*, London: The Industrial Society, 1999, page 110.

[70] See G. Namie and R. Namie, *The Bully at Work: What You Can Do to Stop the Hurt and Reclaim Your Dignity on the Job*, Naperville, Ill.: Sourcebooks, 2000, pages 114–6.

[71] See www.employeeombudsman.sa.gov.au for information on legislation to protect victims of bullying.

[72] See www.bullying.ca for information.

[73] See, for example, Australian Catholic Bishops' Conference and Australian Conference of Leaders of Religious Institutes, *Towards Healing: Principles and Procedures in Responding to Complaints of Abuse Against Personnel of the Catholic Church of Australia, December 2000*, Mordialloc: Centre State Printing, 2000.

[74] See H. Bergson, "Laughter," in the work edited by W. Sypher, *Comedy*, Baltimore: Johns Hopkins, 1956, pages 61–190.

[75] See S. Linstead, "Jokers Wild: Humour in Organizational Culture," in the work edited by C. Powell and G. Patton, *Humour in Society: Resistance and Control*, London: Macmillan, 1988, pages 123–48.

[76] See H. R. Pollio, "What's so Funny?" in the work edited by J. Cherfas and R. Lewin, *Not Work Alone: A Cross-Cultural View of Activities Superfluous to Survival*, London: Temple Smith, 1980, pages 145–64.

[77] See comments by G. M. Smiga, *Pain and Polemic: Anti-Judaism in the Gospels*, New York: Paulist, 1992, pages 63–75.

[78] See R. J. Schreiter, *The Ministry of Reconciliation: Spirituality and Strategies*, Maryknoll: Orbis Books, 2000, pages 55–69.

[79] W. Shakespeare, *Macbeth*, IV, iii, 209.

[80] See J. P. Lederach, *Building Peace: Sustainable Reconciliation in Divided Societies*, Washington, D.C.: U.S. Institute of Peace, 1997, page 29; and Andrew Rigby, *Justice and Reconciliation: After the Violence*, Boulder: Lynne Rienner, 2001, pages 12–3.

[81] Ovid, *Tristia*, book V, eleg. 1, line 63.

[82] See N. C. Habel, *Reconciliation: Searching for Australia's Soul*, Sydney: HarperCollins, 1999, passim.

[83] P. Freire, *Pedagogy of the Oppressed*, New York: Herder and Herder, 1968, page 121.

[84] St. Teresa of Avila is quoted in *Noteworthy: St. Teresa of Avila*, Terre Haute, Ind.: Carmel of St. Joseph, n.d., page 51.

[85] Dorothy Day, quoted by G. A. Vanderhaar, *Beyond Violence*, Mystic, Conn.: Twenty-Third Publications, 1998, page 142.